*There was an Old Derry down Derry,*
*Who loved to see little folks merry;*
  *So he made them a book,*
  *And with laughter they shook*
*At the fun of that Derry down Derry.*

---

**Derry down Derry:** etwa: Juchhe! Kommt in englischen Liedrefrains
vor und ist auch der Name eines der Narren in den volkstümlichen
*Mummers' Plays.* Wegen beider Bedeutungen wählte Lear wohl sein
Pseudonym »Derry down Derry« für die beiden ersten Auflagen seines *Book of Nonsense.* · **folks:** Leute. · **merry:** fröhlich.

3

# 1

There was an Old Man with a beard,
Who said, "It is just as I feared! –
    Two owls and a hen,
    Four larks and a wren,
Have all built their nests in my beard!"

# 2

There was a Young Lady of Ryde,
Whose shoe-strings were seldom untied;
    She purchased some clogs,
    And some small spotty dogs,
And frequently walked about Ryde.

---

1 **owl:** Eule. · **lark:** Lerche. · **wren:** Zaunkönig.
2 **Ryde:** Küstenstadt auf der Isle of Wight. · **untied:** nicht zugebunden. · **to purchase:** kaufen. · **clog:** Holzschuh. · **spotty:** gefleckt. · **frequently:** oft, häufig.

FREMDSPRACHENTEXTE · ENGLISCH

# Edward Lear

# Limericks

Mit Illustrationen
des Autors

Herausgegeben von
Theo Stemmler

Philipp Reclam jun. Stuttgart

RECLAMS UNIVERSAL-BIBLIOTHEK Nr. 19773
Alle Rechte vorbehalten
© 2010 Philipp Reclam jun. GmbH & Co. KG, Stuttgart
Gesamtherstellung: Reclam, Ditzingen. Printed in Germany 2010
RECLAM, UNIVERSAL-BIBLIOTHEK und RECLAMS
UNIVERSAL-BIBLIOTHEK sind eingetragene Marken
der Philipp Reclam jun. GmbH & Co. KG, Stuttgart
ISBN 978-3-15-019773-8

www.reclam.de

### 3

There was an Old Man with a nose,
Who said, "If you choose to suppose,
   That my nose is too long,
    You are certainly wrong!"
That remarkable Man with a nose.


### 4

There was an Old Man on a hill,
Who seldom, if ever, stood still;
   He ran up and down,
    In his Grandmother's gown,
Which adorned that Old Man on a hill.

---

3 **to suppose:** annehmen, vermuten. · **remarkable:** bemerkenswert.
4 **gown:** Kleid. · **to adorn:** schmücken.

**5**

There was a Young Lady whose bonnet,
Came untied when the birds sate upon it;
 But she said, "I don't care!
 All the birds in the air
Are welcome to sit on my bonnet!"

**6**

There was a Young Person of Smyrna,
Whose grandmother threatened to burn her;
 But she seized on the cat,
 And said, "Granny, burn that!
You incongruous Old Woman of Smyrna!"

---

5 **bonnet:** Haube. · **to come untied:** sich lösen. · **sate** (arch.): *sat.*
6 **Smyrna:** griechischer Name der türkischen Stadt Izmir. · **to seize on
s.th.:** sich auf etwas stürzen. · **incongruous:** abwegig.

**7**

There was an Old Person of Chili,
Whose conduct was painful and silly,
    He sate on the stairs,
    Eating apples and pears,
That imprudent Old Person of Chili.

**8**

There was an Old Man with a gong,
Who bumped at it all the day long;
    But they called out, "O law!
    You're a horrid old bore!"
So they smashed that Old Man with a gong.

---

7 **conduct:** Benehmen. · **sate** (arch.): *sat*. · **apples and pears:** Cockney
Rhyming Slang für *stairs*. · **imprudent:** unklug.
8 **to bump at s.th.:** auf etwas schlagen. · **O law!:** *O Lord!* · **horrid:**
schrecklich. · **bore:** Langweiler. · **to smash:** zerschmettern, erschlagen.

**9**

There was an Old Lady of Chertsey,
Who made a remarkable curtsey;
    She twirled round and round,
    Till she sunk underground,
Which distressed all the people of Chertsey.

**10**

There was an Old Man in a tree,
Who was horribly bored by a bee;
    When they said, "Does it buzz?"
    He replied, "Yes, it does!
It's a regular brute of a bee!"

---

9 **Chertsey:** Stadt in Surrey. · **remarkable:** bemerkenswert. · **curtsey:** Knicks. · **to twirl round:** herumwirbeln. · **to distress:** bestürzen.

10 **horribly:** entsetzlich. · **to bore s.o.:** jdn. langweilen. · **to buzz:** summen. · **a regular brute of a bee:** etwa: eine richtig höllische Biene (*brute:* brutaler Kerl; höllische Sache).

## 11

There was an Old Man with a flute,
A sarpint ran into his boot;
   But he played day and night,
   Till the sarpint took flight,
And avoided that man with a flute.

## 12

There was a Young Lady whose chin,
Resembled the point of a pin;
   So she had it made sharp,
   And purchased a harp,
And played several tunes with her chin.

---

11 **flute:** (Quer-)Flöte. · **sarpint:** vulgäre Aussprache von *serpent:* Schlange; Lear verwendet gelegentlich in parodistischer Absicht Eigentümlichkeiten des Londoner Cockney English. Vgl. Anm. zu Nr. 15, 53, 167 und 215.
12 **to resemble:** ähneln. · **to purchase:** kaufen. · **harp:** Harfe. · **tune:** Melodie.

## 13

There was an Old Man of Kilkenny,
Who never had more than a penny;
  He spent all that money,
  In onions and honey,
That wayward Old Man of Kilkenny.

## 14

There was an Old Person of Ischia,
Whose conduct grew friskier and friskier;
  He danced hornpipes and jigs,
  And ate thousands of figs,
That lively Old Person of Ischia.

13 **Kilkenny:** Stadt im Südosten Irlands. · **onion:** Zwiebel. · **wayward:** eigensinnig.
14 **conduct:** Verhalten, Benehmen. · **frisky:** verspielt. · **hornpipes / jigs:** Volkstänze (*jig: gig*). · **fig:** Feige. · **lively:** lebhaft, munter.

**15**

There was an Old Man in a boat,
Who said, "I'm afloat! I'm afloat!"
  When they said, "No! you ain't!"
  He was ready to faint,
That unhappy Old Man in a boat.

**16**

There was a Young Lady of Portugal,
Whose ideas were excessively nautical:
  She climbed up a tree,
  To examine the sea,
But declared she would never leave Portugal.

---

15 **to be afloat:** unter Wasser stehen.  ·  **ain't:** *are not* (s. Anm. zu Nr. 11).  ·  **to faint:** in Ohnmacht fallen.
16 **excessively:** übermäßig.  ·  **nautical:** nautisch, die Seefahrt betreffend.

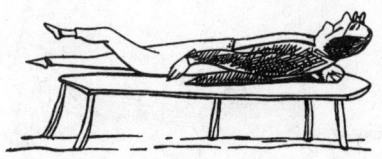

**17**

There was an Old Man of Moldavia,
Who had the most curious behaviour;
   For while he was able,
   He slept on a table.
That funny Old Man of Moldavia.

**18**

There was an Old Man of Madras,
Who rode on a cream-coloured ass;
   But the length of its ears,
   So promoted his fears,
That it killed that Old Man of Madras.

---

17 **Moldavia:** Moldawien; Binnenstaat in Südosteuropa zwischen Rumänien und der Ukraine. · **behaviour:** Verhalten(sweisen).
18 **Madras:** südindische Hafenstadt. · **ass:** Esel. · **to promote:** fördern, verstärken.

**19**

There was an Old Person of Leeds,
Whose head was infested with beads;
   She sat on a stool,
   And ate gooseberry fool,
Which agreed with that person of Leeds.

**20**

There was an Old Man of Peru,
Who never knew what he should do;
   So he tore off his hair,
   And behaved like a bear,
That intrinsic Old Man of Peru.

---

19 **Leeds:** Stadt in Nordengland. · **to be infested with s.th.:** verseucht mit etwas sein. · **bead:** Perle. · **stool:** Hocker, Schemel. · **gooseberry fool:** Stachelbeercreme. · **to agree with s.o.:** jdm. bekommen (Essen).
20 **to behave:** sich verhalten. · **intrinsic:** wesenhaft.

**21**

There was an Old Person of Hurst,
Who drank when he was not athirst;
    When they said, "You'll grow fatter,"
    He answered, "What matter?"
That globular Person of Hurst.

**22**

There was a Young Person of Crete,
Whose toilette was far from complete;
    She dressed in a sack,
    Spickle-speckled with black,
That ombliferous Person of Crete.

---

21 **Hurst:** Stadt in Berkshire. · **athirst:** durstig. · **globular:** kugelförmig.

22 **Crete:** Kreta. · **spickle-speckled:** spielerische Variante von *speckled:* gesprenkelt. · **ombliferous:** unsinnige Wortschöpfung (*-ferous:* -tragend; -phor). Vgl. ähnliche Wortschöpfungen in Nr. 39, 84, 149 und 191.

**23**

There was an Old Man of the Isles,
Whose face was pervaded with smiles:
   He sung "High dum diddle,"
   And played on the fiddle,
That amiable Man of the Isles.

**24**

There was an Old Person of Buda,
Whose conduct grew ruder and ruder;
   Till at last, with a hammer,
   They silenced his clamour,
By smashing that Person of Buda.

---

23 **the Isles:** Sammelbegriff für die schottischen Inseln. · **to be pervaded with s.th.:** mit etwas durchsetzt sein. · **fiddle:** Geige. · **amiable:** liebenswürdig.
24 **Buda:** westlich der Donau gelegener Stadtteil von Budapest. · **conduct:** Benehmen, Betragen, Verhalten. · **clamour:** Lärm, Geschrei. · **to smash:** zerschmettern, erschlagen.

**25**

There was an Old Man of Columbia,
Who was thirsty, and called out for some beer;
    But they brought it quite hot,
    In a small copper pot,
Which disgusted that man of Columbia.

**26**

There was a Young Lady of Dorking,
Who bought a large bonnet for walking;
    But its colour and size,
    So bedazzled her eyes,
That she very soon went back to Dorking.

---

25 **Columbia: 1.** weibliche Personifikation der USA (nach *Christopher Columbus*); **2.** Name mehrerer US-amerikanischer Städte, so etwa der Hauptstadt des Bundesstaats South Carolina. · **copper:** Kupfer. · **to disgust:** anekeln, anwidern.

26 **Dorking:** Ort in Surrey südlich von London. · **bonnet:** Haube. · **to bedazzle:** blenden.

**27**

There was an Old Man who supposed,
That the street door was partially closed;
   But some very large rats,
   Ate his coats and his hats,
While that futile old gentleman dozed.

**28**

There was an Old Man of the West,
Who wore a pale plum-coloured vest;
   When they said, "Does it fit?"
   He replied, "Not a bit!"
That uneasy Old Man of the West.

---

27 **to suppose:** annehmen, vermuten. · **partially:** teilweise. · **futile:** vergeblich (handelnd). · **to doze:** dösen, ein Nickerchen machen.
28 **plum-coloured:** pflaumenfarben. · **vest:** Weste. · **uneasy:** beunruhigt.

**29**

There was an Old Man of the Wrekin
Whose shoes made a horrible creaking.
    But they said, "Tell us whether,
    Your shoes are of leather,
Or of what, you Old Man of the Wrekin?"

**30**

There was a Young Lady whose eyes,
Were unique as to colour and size;
    When she opened them wide,
    People all turned aside,
And started away in surprise.

---

29 **Wrekin:** Berg im Osten von Shropshire. · **horrible:** entsetzlich. ·
    **creaking:** Knarren.
30 **unique:** einzigartig. · **to start away:** weglaufen.

**31**

There was a Young Lady of Norway,
Who casually sat in a doorway;
　　When the door squeezed her flat,
　　She exclaimed, "What of that?"
This courageous Young Lady of Norway.

**32**

There was an Old Man of Vienna,
Who lived upon Tincture of Senna;
　　When that did not agree,
　　He took Camomile Tea,
That nasty Old Man of Vienna.

---

31 **casually:** lässig. · **to squeeze:** quetschen, drücken. · **what of that?:** na und? · **courageous:** mutig.
32 **Vienna:** Wien. · **tincture of senna:** Aufguss von Sennesblättern (Abführmittel). · **to agree:** bekömmlich, zuträglich sein. · **camomile tea:** Kamillentee. · **nasty:** garstig.

**33**

There was an Old Person whose habits,
Induced him to feed upon rabbits;
   When he'd eaten eighteen,
   He turned perfectly green,
Upon which he relinquished those habits.

**34**

There was an Old Person of Dover,
Who rushed through a field of blue clover;
   But some very large bees,
   Stung his nose and his knees,
So he very soon went back to Dover.

---

33 **to induce s.o. to do s.th.:** jdn. dazu verleiten, etwas zu tun. · **to feed upon s.th.:** sich von etwas ernähren. · **to relinquish:** aufgeben.
34 **clover:** Klee. · **to sting** (*stung, stung*): stechen.

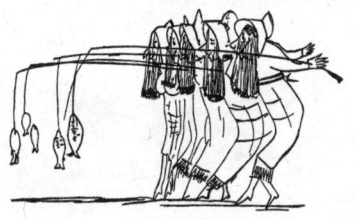

### 35

There was an Old Man of Marseilles,
Whose daughters wore bottle-green veils;
   They caught several fish,
   Which they put in a dish,
And sent to their Pa' at Marseilles.

### 36

There was an Old Person of Cadiz,
Who was always polite to all ladies;
   But in handling his daughter,
   He fell into the water,
Which drowned that Old Person of Cadiz.

---

35 **veil:** Schleier.
36 **Cadiz:** südwestspanische Hafenstadt. · **to handle s.o.:** mit jdm. umgehen. · **to drown s.o.:** jdn. ertränken.

**37**

There was an Old Person of Basing,
Whose presence of mind was amazing;
   He purchased a steed,
   Which he rode at full speed,
And escaped from the people of Basing.

**38**

There was an Old Man of Quebec,
A beetle ran over his neck;
   But he cried, "With a needle,
   I'll slay you, O beadle!"
That angry Old Man of Quebec.

37 **Basing:** Gemeinde im Nordosten von Hampshire. · **presence of
mind:** Geistesgegenwart. · **amazing:** erstaunlich. · **to purchase:**
kaufen. · **steed:** Ross.
38 **Quebec:** Stadt in Kanada. · **beetle:** Käfer. · **to slay:** erschlagen, er-
legen. · **beadle:** Kirchendiener (kalauerndes Wortspiel).

### 39

There was an Old Person of Philae,
Whose conduct was scroobious and wily;
   He rushed up a palm,
   When the weather was calm,
And observed all the ruins of Philae.

### 40

There was a Young Lady of Bute,
Who played on a silver-gilt flute;
   She played several jigs,
   To her uncle's white pigs,
That amusing Young Lady of Bute.

---

39 **Philae:** Tempelkomplex in Oberägypten. · **conduct:** Benehmen. ·
**scroobious:** von Lear erfundenes Nonsense-Wort, zusammenge-
setzt aus *scurrilous* ›skurril‹, *curious* ›seltsam‹, *dubious* ›zweifel-
haft‹; vgl. Nr. 22, 84 und 149. · **wily:** schlau.
40 **Bute:** Grafschaft im Südwesten Schottlands. · **silver-gilt:** aus ver-
goldetem Silber. · **flute:** (Quer-)Flöte. · **jig:** *gig:* Volkstanz.

**41**

There was a Young Lady whose nose,
Was so long that it reached to her toes;
   So she hired an Old Lady,
   Whose conduct was steady,
To carry that wonderful nose.

**42**

There was a Young Lady of Turkey,
Who wept when the weather was murky;
   When the day turned out fine,
   She ceased to repine,
That capricious Young Lady of Turkey.

---

41 **conduct:** Verhalten. · **steady:** ruhig; standhaft.
42 **murky:** trübe. · **to cease:** aufhören. · **to repine:** klagen. · **capricious:** launisch.

**43**

There was an Old Man of Apulia,
Whose conduct was very peculiar;
   He fed twenty sons,
   Upon nothing but buns,
That whimsical Man of Apulia.

**44**

There was an Old Man with a poker,
Who painted his face with red oker;
   When they said, "You're a guy!"
   He made no reply,
But knocked them all down with his poker.

---

43 **Apulia:** Apulien; süditalienische Region. · **conduct:** Verhalten. ·
**peculiar:** seltsam. · **to feed** (*fed*, *fed*) **s.o. upon s.th.:** jdn. mit etwas
füttern, ernähren. · **bun:** süßes Brötchen. · **whimsical:** wunderlich.
44 **poker:** Schürhaken. · **oker:** *ochre:* Ocker. · **guy** (infml.): Kerl.

**45**

There was an Old Person of Prague,
Who was suddenly seized with the plague;
   But they gave him some butter,
   Which caused him to mutter,
And cured that Old Person of Prague.

**46**

There was an Old Man of the North,
Who fell into a basin of broth;
   But a laudable cook,
   Fished him out with a hook,
Which saved that Old Man of the North.

---

45 **plague:** Pest. · **to mutter:** murmeln; murren.
46 **basin of broth:** Kessel voll (heißer) Brühe. · **laudable:** lobenswert.

**47**

There was a Young Lady of Poole,
Whose soup was excessively cool;
   So she put it to boil
   By the aid of some oil,
That ingenious Young Lady of Poole.

**48**

There was an Old Person of Mold,
Who shrank from sensations of cold;
   So he purchased some muffs,
   Some furs and some fluffs,
And wrapped himself from the cold.

---

47 **Poole:** englische Küstenstadt am Ärmelkanal. · **excessively:** übermäßig. · **ingenious:** erfinderisch.
48 **Mold:** Ortschaft in Wales. · **to shrink** (*shrank, shrank*) **from s.th.:**
vor etwas zurückschrecken. · **sensation:** Empfindung. · **to purchase:** kaufen. · **muff:** Muff. · **fluff:** Flaum. · **to wrap o.s.:** sich
einhüllen.

**49**

There was an Old Man of Nepaul,
From his horse had a terrible fall;
    But, though split quite in two,
    By some very strong glue,
They mended that Man of Nepaul.

**50**

There was an Old Man of th' Abruzzi,
So blind that he couldn't his foot see;
    When they said, "That's your toe,"
    He replied, "Is it so?"
That doubtful Old Man of th' Abruzzi.

---

49 **Nepaul:** Nepal. · **glue:** Leim. · **to mend:** reparieren.
50 **Abruzzi** (pl.): die Abruzzen; italienischer Gebirgszug. · **doubtful:**
   skeptisch; zweifelnd.

**51**

There was an Old Person of Rhodes,
Who strongly objected to toads;
   He paid several cousins,
   To catch them by dozens,
That futile Old Person of Rhodes.

**52**

There was an Old Man of Peru,
Who watched his wife making a stew;
   But once by mistake,
   In a stove she did bake,
That unfortunate Man of Peru.

---

51 **Rhodes:** Rhodos. · **to object to s.th.:** sich an etwas stören, etwas gegen etwas haben. · **toad:** Kröte. · **futile:** hier: vergeblich (handelnd); zum Scheitern verurteilt.
52 **stew:** Eintopf. · **stove:** (Back-)Ofen.

### 53

There was an Old Man of Melrose,
Who walked on the tips of his toes;
   But they said, "It ain't pleasant,
   To see you at present,
You stupid Old Man of Melrose."

### 54

There was a Young Lady of Lucca,
Whose lovers completely forsook her;
   She ran up a tree,
   And said, "Fiddle-de-dee!"
Which embarrassed the people of Lucca.

---

53 **Melrose:** Stadt im schottischen Grenzland. · **ain't:** *is not*; s. Anm.
zu Nr. 11 und vgl. Nr. 15 und 167.
54 **Lucca:** italienische Stadt in der westlichen Toskana. · **to forsake**
(*forsook, forsaken*): verlassen. · **to embarrass:** verlegen machen.

**55**

There was an Old Man of Bohemia,
Whose daughter was christened Euphemia;
   Till one day, to his grief,
   She married a thief,
Which grieved that Old Man of Bohemia.

**56**

There was an Old Man of Vesuvius,
Who studied the works of Vitruvius;
   When the flames burnt his book,
   To drinking he took,
That morbid Old Man of Vesuvius.

---

55 **Bohemia:** Böhmen. · **to christen s.o.:** jdn. taufen. · **grief:** Kummer. · **to grieve:** bekümmern.
56 **Vitruvius:** Militärtechniker und Ingenieur zur Zeit Cäsars. · **to take to s.th.:** einer Sache verfallen. · **morbid:** morbid, kränklich.

There was an Old Man of Cape Horn,
Who wished he had never been born;
    So he sat on a chair,
    Till he died of despair,
That dolorous Man of Cape Horn.

**58**

There was an Old Lady whose folly,
Induced her to sit in a holly;
    Whereon by a thorn,
    Her dress being torn,
She quickly became melancholy.

---

57 **Cape Horn:** Kap Hoorn; Landspitze in Chile (südlichster Punkt Südamerikas). · **despair:** Verzweiflung. · **dolorous:** traurig.
58 **folly:** Torheit. · **to induce s.o. to do s.th.:** jdn. dazu verleiten, etwas zu tun. · **holly:** Stechpalme.

**59**

There was an Old Man of Corfu,
Who never knew what he should do;
  So he rushed up and down,
  Till the sun made him brown,
That bewildered Old Man of Corfu.


**60**

There was an Old Man of the South,
Who had an immoderate mouth;
  But in swallowing a dish,
  That was quite full of fish,
He was choked, that Old Man of the South.


59 **Corfu:** griechische Insel. · **bewildered:** verwirrt.
60 **immoderate mouth:** maßloser Appetit. · **to swallow:** verschlingen. · **to choke:** ersticken.

**61**

There was an Old Man of the Nile,
Who sharpened his nails with a file;
   Till he cut off his thumbs,
    And said calmly, "This comes –
Of sharpening one's nails with a file!"

**62**

There was an Old Person of Rheims,
Who was troubled with horrible dreams;
   So, to keep him awake,
    They fed him with cake.
Which amused that Old Person of Rheims.

---

61 **file:** Feile.
62 **Rheims:** Reims; Stadt in Nordfrankreich. · **horrible:** schrecklich.

**63**

There was an Old Person of Cromer,
Who stood on one leg to read Homer;
　　When he found he grew stiff,
　　He jumped over the cliff,
Which concluded that Person of Cromer.

**64**

There was an Old Person of Troy,
Whose drink was warm brandy and soy;
　　Which he took with a spoon,
　　By the light of the moon,
In sight of the city of Troy.

---

63 **Cromer:** Stadt an der Nordküste von Norfolk. · **stiff:** steif. · **to**
　　**conclude:** ein Ende machen.
64 **Troy:** Troja. · **soy:** Soja.

**65**

There was an Old Man of the Dee,
Who was sadly annoyed by a flea;
    When he said, "I will scratch it" –
    They gave him a hatchet,
Which grieved that Old Man of the Dee.

**66**

There was an Old Man of Dundee,
Who frequented the top of a tree;
    When disturbed by the crows,
    He abruptly arose,
And exclaimed, "I'll return to Dundee."

65 **Dee: 1.** Fluss in Schottland; **2.** Fluss in Wales. · **to annoy s.o.:** jdn. belästigen, ärgern. · **flea:** Floh. · **to scratch:** kratzen. · **hatchet:** Beil. · **to grieve:** betrüben.
66 **Dundee:** Stadt in Schottland. · **to frequent:** häufig besuchen. · **to disturb s.o.:** jdn. stören. · **crow:** Krähe. · **to arise** (*arose, arisen*): aufstehen.

**67**

There was an Old Person of Tring,
Who embellished his nose with a ring;
    He gazed at the moon,
    Every evening in June,
That ecstatic Old Person of Tring.

**68**

There was an Old Man on some rocks,
Who shut his wife up in a box,
    When she said, "Let me out,"
    He exclaimed, "Without doubt,
You will pass all your life in that box."

---

67 **Tring:** Gemeinde in den Chiltern Hills (England). · **to embellish:** verschönern. · **to gaze at s.th.:** etwas anstarren. · **ecstatic:** verzückt.

**69**

There was an Old Man of Coblenz,
The length of whose legs was immense;
   He went with one prance,
   From Turkey to France,
That surprising Old Man of Coblenz.

**70**

There was an Old Man of Calcutta,
Who perpetually ate bread and butter;
   Till a great bit of muffin,
   On which he was stuffing,
Choked that horrid Old Man of Calcutta.

---

69 **prance:** Sprung.
70 **perpetually:** ständig. · **to stuff:** sich vollstopfen. · **to choke:** ersticken. · **horrid:** schrecklich.

**71**

There was an Old Man in a pew,
Whose waistcoat was spotted with blue;
   But he tore it in pieces,
   To give to his nieces, –
That cheerful Old Man in a pew.

**72**

There was an Old Man who said – "How,
Shall I flee from this horrible cow?
   I will sit on this stile,
   And continue to smile,
Which may soften the heart of that cow."

---

71 **pew:** Kirchenstuhl. · **waistcoat:** Wams, Weste. · **spotted:** getüp-
felt. · **cheerful:** fröhlich.
72 **to flee from s.th.:** vor etwas fliehen. · **horrible:** schrecklich. · **stile:**
Gatter.

**73**

There was a Young Lady of Hull,
Who was chased by a virulent bull;
   But she seized on a spade,
   And called out – "Who's afraid!"
Which distracted that virulent bull.

**74**

There was an Old Man of Whitehaven,
Who danced a quadrille with a raven;
   But they said – "It's absurd,
   To encourage this bird!"
So they smashed that Old Man of Whitehaven.

---

73 **Hull:** Stadt in Nordostengland. · **to chase s.o.:** jdn. jagen. · **virulent:** bösartig. · **spade:** Spaten. · **to distract:** ablenken.
74 **Whitehaven:** Hafenstadt in Nordostengland. · **quadrille:** von vier Personen im Karree getanzter Kontertanz. · **raven:** Rabe. · **to encourage:** ermuntern. · **to smash:** zerschmettern, vernichten.

40

**75**

There was an Old Man of Leghorn,
The smallest as ever was born;
  But quickly snapt up he,
  Was once by a puppy,
Who devoured that Old Man of Leghorn.

**76**

There was an Old Man of the Hague,
Whose ideas were excessively vague;
  He built a balloon,
  To examine the moon,
That deluded Old Man of the Hague.

---

75 **Leghorn:** Livorno; italienische Stadt an der ligurischen Küste. • **to snap:** schnappen. • **puppy:** junger Hund. • **to devour:** verschlingen.
76 **the Hague:** *The Hague:* Den Haag. • **excessively:** übermäßig. • **deluded:** irregeleitet.

**77**

There was an Old Man of Jamaica,
Who suddenly married a Quaker!
   But she cried out – "O lack!
   I have married a black!"
Which distressed that Old Man of Jamaica.

**78**

There was an Old Person of Dutton,
Whose head was so small as a button:
   So to make it look big,
   He purchased a wig,
And rapidly rushed about Dutton.

---

77 **quaker:** Angehörige(r) einer Kirche und Dogma ablehnenden christlichen Gemeinschaft. · **O lack!:** Oje! · **to distress:** bekümmern.

78 **Dutton:** Stadt im US-amerikanischen Bundesstaat Montana. · **to purchase:** kaufen. · **wig:** Perücke. · **rapidly:** geschwind.

**79**

There was a Young Lady of Tyre,
Who swept the loud chords of a lyre;
    At the sound of each sweep,
    She enraptured the deep,
And enchanted the city of Tyre.

**80**

There was an Old Man who said, "Hush!
I perceive a young bird in this bush!"
    When they said – "Is it small?"
    He replied – "Not at all!
It is four times as big as the bush!"

---

79 **Tyre:** Tyros; südlibanesische Stadt. · **to sweep:** kehren, fegen. ·
**chords of a lyre:** Lyra-Saiten. · **to enrapture:** bezaubern. · **deep:**
Meer. · **to enchant:** verzaubern.
80 **hush!:** pst! · **to perceive:** wahrnehmen.

**81**

There was an Old Man of the East,
Who gave all his children a feast;
  But they all ate so much,
  And their conduct was such,
That it killed that Old Man of the East.


**82**

There was an Old Man of Kamschatka,
Who possessed a remarkably fat cur.
  His gait and his waddle,
  Were held as a model,
To all the fat dogs in Kamschatka.

81 **feast:** Festmahl. · **conduct:** Benehmen.
82 **Kamschatka:** fälschlich für *Kamchatka:* Halbinsel in Nordostsibiri-
  en. · **remarkably:** bemerkenswert. · **cur:** Köter. · **gait:** Gang. ·
  **waddle:** Watscheln.

44

**83**

There was an Old Man of the Coast,
Who placidly sat on a post;
    But when it was cold,
    He relinquished his hold,
And called for some hot buttered toast.

**84**

There was an Old Person of Bangor,
Whose face was distorted with anger,
    He tore off his boots,
    And subsisted on roots,
That borascible Person of Bangor.

---

83 **placidly:** ruhig. · **post:** Pfosten. · **to relinquish:** verlassen.
84 **Bangor:** Stadt im Nordwesten von Wales. · **to distort:** verzerren. ·
**anger:** Zorn. · **to subsist on s.th.:** sich von etwas ernähren. · **boras-cible:** Wortschöpfung; Wortspiel mit *irascible* ›jähzornig‹ (vgl. Nr. 22 und 39).

**85**

There was an Old Man with a beard,
Who sat on a horse when he reared;
   But they said, "Never mind!
   You will fall off behind,
You propitious Old Man with a beard!"

**86**

There was an Old Man of the West,
Who never could get any rest;
   So they set him to spin,
   On his nose and his chin,
Which cured that Old Man of the West.

---

85 **to rear:** sich aufbäumen. · **propitious:** günstig; hier etwa: glücklich.
86 **to spin:** sich drehen.

**87**

There was an Old Person of Anerley,
Whose conduct was strange and unmannerly;
   He rushed down the Strand,
   With a pig in each hand,
But returned in the evening to Anerley.

**88**

There was a Young Lady of Troy,
Whom several large flies did annoy;
   Some she killed with a thump,
   Some she drowned at the pump,
And some she took with her to Troy.

---

87 **Anerley:** Vorort von London. · **conduct:** Verhalten. · **unmannerly:**
unschicklich. · **Strand:** belebte Straße in London, die das Westend
mit der City verbindet.
88 **Troy:** Troja. · **to annoy:** ärgern, belästigen. · **thump:** Schlag. · **to
drown:** ertränken.

**89**

There was an Old Man of Berlin,
Whose form was uncommonly thin;
 Till he once, by mistake,
 Was mixed up in a cake,
So they baked that Old Man of Berlin.

**90**

There was an Old Person of Spain,
Who hated all trouble and pain;
 So he sate on a chair,
 With his feet in the air,
That umbrageous Old Person of Spain.

90 **sate** (arch.): *sat.* · **umbrageous:** schattenspendend.

48

**91**

There was a Young Lady of Russia,
Who screamed so that no one could hush her;
   Her screams were extreme,
   No one heard such a scream,
As was screamed by that Lady of Russia.

**92**

There was an Old Man who said, "Well!
Will *nobody* answer this bell?
   I have pulled day and night,
   Till my hair has grown white,
But nobody answers this bell!"

---

91 **to scream:** schreien, kreischen. · **to hush:** zum Schweigen bringen.
92 **to answer the bell:** die Tür öffnen.

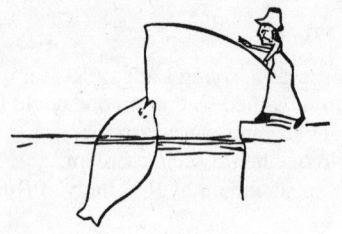

**93**

There was a Young Lady of Wales,
Who caught a large fish without scales;
   When she lifted her hook,
   She exclaimed, "Only look!"
That ecstatic Young Lady of Wales.

**94**

There was an Old Person of Cheadle,
Was put in the stocks by the beadle;
   For stealing some pigs,
   Some coats and some wigs,
That horrible Person of Cheadle.

---

93 **scale:** Schuppe. · **ecstatic:** ekstatisch, begeistert.
94 **Cheadle:** Ort in Staffordshire. · **stocks** (pl.): Gestell aus Holzblö-
   cken oder Metall, in das im Mittelalter ein Verurteilter an Händen
   und Füßen eingeschlossen wurde. · **beadle:** Gerichtsbüttel. · **wig:**
   Perücke. · **horrible:** schrecklich.

**95**

There was a Young Lady of Welling,
Whose praise all the world was a telling;
  She played on the harp,
  And caught several carp,
That accomplished Young Lady of Welling.

**96**

There was an Old Person of Tartary,
Who divided his jugular artery;
  But he screeched to his wife,
  And she said, "Oh, my life!
Your death will be felt by all Tartary!"

---

95 **Welling:** Vorort von London. · **a telling:** *a-telling* (arch.): *telling*. ·
**harp:** Harfe. · **carp:** Karpfen. · **accomplished:** vollendet; hier etwa:
vielseitig.
96 **Tartary:** fälschlich für *Tatary:* alte Bezeichnung für Tatarstan, auto-
nome Republik im östlichen Teil des europäischen Russland. ·
**jugular artery:** Halsarterie. · **to screech:** kreischen.

**97**

There was an Old Person of Chester,
Whom several small children did pester;
   They threw some large stones,
   Which broke most of his bones,
And displeased that Old Person of Chester.

**98**

There was an Old Man with an owl,
Who continued to bother and howl;
   He sate on a rail,
   And imbibed bitter ale,
Which refreshed that Old Man and his owl.

---

97 **Chester:** Stadt in Nordwestengland an der Grenze zu Wales. · **to pester:** belästigen. · **to displease:** missfallen.

98 **owl:** Eule. · **to bother:** belästigen. · **to howl:** heulen. · **sate** (arch.): *sat*. · **rail:** Geländer. · **to imbibe** (hum.): trinken. · **to refresh:** erfrischen.

**99**

There was an Old Person of Gretna,
Who rushed down the crater of Etna;
    When they said, "Is it hot?"
    He replied, "No, it's not!"
That mendacious Old Person of Gretna.

**100**

There was a Young Lady of Sweden,
Who went by the slow train to Weedon;
    When they cried, "Weedon Station!"
    She made no observation,
But she thought she should go back to Sweden.

---

99 **Gretna:** *Gretna Green:* Ort in Südschottland. · **Etna:** der Ätna;
Vulkan auf Sizilien. · **mendacious:** verlogen.
100 **Weedon:** Gemeinde in Northamptonshire. · **observation:** Bemerkung.

**101**

There was a Young Girl of Majorca,
Whose aunt was a very fast walker;
   She walked seventy miles,
   And leaped fifteen stiles,
Which astonished that Girl of Majorca.

**102**

There was an Old Man of the Cape,
Who possessed a large barbary ape;
   Till the ape one dark night,
   Set the house on a light,
Which burned that Old Man of the Cape.

---

101 **to leap:** überspringen. · **stile:** Gatter.
102 **the Cape:** *the Cape of Good Hope:* das Kap der Guten Hoffnung;
    Kap im Süden der Kaphalbinsel (Republik Südafrika). · **barbary
    ape:** Berberaffe.

**103**

There was an Old Lady of Prague,
Whose language was horribly vague.
　　When they said, "Are these caps?"
　　She answered, "Perhaps!"
That oracular Lady of Prague.

**104**

There was an Old Person of Sparta,
Who had twenty-five sons and one daughter;
　　He fed them on snails,
　　And weighed them in scales,
That wonderful Person of Sparta.

---

103 **horribly:** schrecklich. · **oracular:** orakelhaft.
104 **daughter:** Die Aussprache /dɑːtə/ ist eine vulgäre Variante (vgl. Anm. zu Nr. 11). · **to feed** (*fed, fed*) **s.o. on s.th.:** jdn. mit etwas füttern, ernähren. · **snail:** Schnecke. · **scales** (pl.): Waage.

## 105

There was an Old Man at a casement,
Who held up his hands in amazement;
   When they said, "Sir! you'll fall!"
   He replied, "Not at all!"
That incipient Old Man at a casement.

## 106

There was an Old Person of Burton,
Whose answers were rather uncertain;
   When they said, "How d'ye do?"
   He replied, "Who are you?"
That distressing Old Person of Burton.

---

105 **casement:** Fensterflügel. · **amazement:** Verwunderung. · **incipient:** anfänglich (gibt hier keinen Sinn).
106 **Burton:** Stadt im Osten von Staffordshire. · **distressing:** besorgniserregend.

**107**

There was an Old Person of Ems,
Who casually fell in the Thames;
   And when he was found,
   They said he was drowned,
That unlucky Old Person of Ems.

**108**

There was an Old Person of Ewell,
Who chiefly subsisted on gruel;
   But to make it more nice,
   He inserted some mice,
Which refreshed that Old Person of Ewell.

---

107 **Ems:** eigtl.: Fluss im Nordwesten Deutschlands und Nordosten
    der Niederlande; gemeint ist vielleicht das Emsland oder Bad
    Ems. · **casually:** zufällig, aus Versehen. · **drowned:** ertrunken.
108 **Ewell:** Ort in Surrey. · **to subsist on s.th.:** sich von etwas ernäh-
    ren. · **gruel:** Haferschleim. · **to insert:** einfügen, dazutun. · **to**
    **refresh:** erfrischen.

**109**

There was a Young Lady of Parma,
Whose conduct grew calmer and calmer;
 When they said, "Are you dumb?"
 She merely said, "Hum!"
That provoking Young Lady of Parma.

**110**

There was an Old Man of Aôsta,
Who possessed a large cow, but he lost her;
 But they said, "Don't you see,
 She has rushed up a tree?
You invidious Old Man of Aôsta!"

---

109 **Parma:** italienische Stadt in der Emilia Romagna. · **conduct:** Verhalten. · **dumb:** stumm. · **merely:** bloß. · **provoking:** provozierend.
110 **Aôsta:** *Aosta:* Hauptstadt der italienischen Region Aostatal. · **invidious:** boshaft.

**111**

There was an Old Man, on whose nose,
Most birds of the air could repose;
   But they all flew away,
   At the closing of day,
Which relieved that Old Man and his nose.

**112**

There was a Young Lady of Clare,
Who was madly pursued by a bear;
   When she found she was tired,
   She abruptly expired,
That unfortunate Lady of Clare.

111 **to repose:** sich ausruhen. · **to relieve:** erleichtern.
112 **Clare:** irische Grafschaft. · **to pursue s.o.:** jdn. verfolgen. · **to expire:** verscheiden.

**113**

There was an Old Man of Hong Kong,
Who never did anything wrong;
 He lay on his back,
 With his head in a sack,
That innocuous Old Man of Hong Kong.

**114**

There was an Old Person of Fife,
Who was greatly disgusted with life;
 They sang him a ballad,
 And fed him on salad,
Which cured that Old Person of Fife.

---

113 **innocuous:** unschuldig.
114 **Fife:** schottische Region. · **to be disgusted with s.th.:** von etwas
angewidert sein. · **to feed** (*fed*, *fed*) **s.o. on s.th.:** jdn. mit etwas ernähren.

**115**

There was a Young Person in green,
Who seldom was fit to be seen;
  She wore a long shawl,
  Over bonnet and all,
Which enveloped that Person in green.

**116**

There was an Old Person of Slough,
Who danced at the end of a bough;
  But they said, "If you sneeze,
  You might damage the trees,
You imprudent Old Person of Slough."

---

115 **to be fit to be seen:** sich sehen lassen können. · **shawl:** Umhang. ·
**bonnet:** Haube. · **to envelop:** umhüllen.
116 **Slough:** Stadt in Berkshire. · **bough:** Zweig. · **to sneeze:** niesen. ·
**imprudent:** unvorsichtig.

**117**

There was an Old Person of Putney,
Whose food was roast spiders and chutney,
   Which he took with his tea,
   Within sight of the sea,
That romantic Old Person of Putney.


**118**

There was a Young Lady in white,
Who looked out at the depths of the night;
   But the birds of the air,
   Filled her heart with despair,
And oppressed that Young Lady in white.

---

117 **Putney:** Stadtteil von London. · **chutney:** scharf gewürzte Paste
     aus Früchten.
118 **despair:** Verzweiflung. · **to oppress:** bedrücken.

**119**

There was an Old Person of Brill,
Who purchased a shirt with a frill;
  But they said, "Don't you wish,
  You mayn't look like a fish,
You obsequious Old Person of Brill?"

**120**

There was an Old Man of Three Bridges,
Whose mind was distracted by midges,
  He sate on a wheel,
  Eating underdone veal,
Which relieved that Old Man of Three Bridges.

---

119 **Brill:** Ort in Buckinghamshire. · **to purchase:** kaufen. · **frill:** Rü-
    sche. · **obsequious:** unterwürfig (gibt hier keinen Sinn).
120 **Three Bridges:** Gemeinde in West Sussex. · **to distract:** ablen-
    ken. · **midge:** Mücke. · **sate** (arch.): *sat*. · **underdone veal:** nicht
    gares Kalbfleisch. · **to relieve:** erleichtern.

63

**121**

There was an Old Person of Wick,
Who said, "Tick-a-Tick, Tick-a-Tick;
  Chickabee, Chickabaw,"
   And he said nothing more,
That laconic Old Person of Wick.


**122**

There was a Young Lady in blue,
Who said, "Is it you? Is it you?"
  When they said, "Yes, it is," –
  She replied only, "Whizz!"
That ungracious Young Lady in blue.

---

121 **Wick:** schottische Hafenstadt; auch: Ort in Gloucestershire. · **laconic:** lakonisch, kurz angebunden.
122 **whizz!:** etwa: pah! · **ungracious:** unhöflich.

**123**

There was an Old Person of China,
Whose daughters were Jiska and Dinah,
    Amelia and Fluffy,
    Olivia and Chuffy,
And all of them settled in China.

**124**

There was an Old Man of the Dargle
Who purchased six barrels of Gargle;
    For he said, "I'll sit still,
    And will roll them downhill,
For the fish in the depths of the Dargle."

---

123 **to settle:** sich niederlassen.
124 **Dargle:** Fluss in Irland. · **to purchase:** kaufen. · **gargle:** Gurgel-
wasser.

There was an Old Man in a Marsh,
Whose manners were futile and harsh;
   He sate on a log,
   And sang songs to a frog,
That instructive Old Man in a Marsh.

**126**

There was a Young Person in red,
Who carefully covered her head,
   With a bonnet of leather,
   And three lines of feather,
Besides some long ribands of red.

---

125 **marsh:** Sumpf. · **futile:** nutzlos. · **harsh:** rücksichtslos. · **sate**
(arch.): *sat.* · **log:** Baumstamm. · **instructive:** lehrreich.
126 **bonnet:** Haube. · **riband:** Band.

**127**

There was an Old Person of Bree,
Who frequented the depths of the sea;
   She nurs'd the small fishes,
   And washed all the dishes,
And swam back again into Bree.

**128**

There was an Old Man in a barge,
Whose nose was exceedingly large;
   But in fishing by night,
   It supported a light,
Which helped that Old Man in a barge.

127 **Bree:** Stadt in Belgien. · **to frequent:** häufig aufsuchen.
128 **barge:** Barke. · **exceedingly:** äußerst. · **to support:** stützen.

**129**

There was an Old Person in black,
A grasshopper jumped on his back;
 When it chirped in his ear,
 He was smitten with fear,
That helpless Old Person in black.

**130**

There was an Old Man of Toulouse
Who purchased a new pair of shoes;
 When they asked, "Are they pleasant?" –
 He said, "Not at present!"
That turbid Old Man of Toulouse.

---

129 **to chirp:** zirpen. · **to be smitten with s.th.:** von etwas ergriffen
 sein.
130 **to purchase:** kaufen. · **turbid:** verwirrt.

68

### 131

There was an Old Man of Blackheath,
Whose head was adorned with a wreath,
  Of lobsters and spice,
  Pickled onions and mice,
That uncommon Old Man of Blackheath.

### 132

There was an Old Man on the Humber,
Who dined on a cake of burnt Umber;
  When he said – "It's enough!" –
  They only said, "Stuff!
You amazing Old Man on the Humber!"

---

131 **Blackheath:** Stadtteil von London. · **to adorn:** schmücken. ·
**wreath:** Kranz. · **lobster:** Hummer. · **spice:** Gewürz(kraut). ·
**pickled onions:** eingelegte Zwiebeln.
132 **Humber:** Fluss in England. · **burnt umber:** Umbra (dunkelbraune
Farbe). · **to stuff:** sich vollstopfen. · **amazing:** erstaunlich.

### 133

There was an Old Person of Stroud,
Who was horribly jammed in a crowd;
   Some she slew with a kick,
   Some she scrunched with a stick,
That impulsive Old Person of Stroud.

### 134

There was an Old Man of Boulak,
Who sate on a crocodile's back;
   But they said, "Tow'rds the night,
   He may probably bite,
Which might vex you, Old Man of Boulak!"

---

133 **Stroud:** Stadt in Gloucestershire. · **horribly:** entsetzlich. ·
**jammed:** eingekeilt. · **to slay** (*slew, slain*): erschlagen. · **to scrunch:**
zermalmen.
134 **Boulak:** Hafen von Kairo. · **sate** (arch.): *sat.* · **to vex:** ärgern.

### 135

There was an Old Man of Ibreem,
Who suddenly threaten'd to scream:
  But they said, "If you do,
  We will thump you quite blue,
You disgusting Old Man of Ibreem!"

### 136

There was an Old Lady of France,
Who taught little ducklings to dance;
  When she said, "Tick-a-tack!" –
  They only said, "Quack!"
Which grieved that Old Lady of France.

---

135 **Ibreem:** Ort in Ägypten. · **to scream:** schreien. · **to thump:** verdreschen. · **disgusting:** abstoßend, widerlich.
136 **to grieve:** betrüben.

**137**

There was an Old Man who screamed out
Whenever they knocked him about;
  So they took off his boots,
  And fed him with fruits,
And continued to knock him about.

**138**

There was an Old Person of Woking,
Whose mind was perverse and provoking;
  He sate on a rail,
  With his head in a pail,
That illusive Old Person of Woking.

137 **to scream out:** losschreien.
138 **Woking:** Stadt in Surrey. · **provoking:** provozierend. · **sate**
(arch): *sat*. · **rail:** Geländer. · **pail:** Eimer. · **illusive:** illusorisch
(gibt hier keinen Sinn).

**139**

There was a Young Person of Bantry,
Who frequently slept in the pantry;
    When disturbed by the mice,
    She appeased them with rice
That judicious Young Person of Bantry.

**140**

There was an Old Man at a junction,
Whose feelings were wrung with compunction,
    When they said, "The Train's gone!"
    He exclaimed, "How forlorn!"
But remained on the rails of the junction.

---

139 **Bantry:** Stadt im Südwesten Irlands. · **frequently:** häufig. · **pantry:** Speisekammer. · **to disturb s.o.:** jdn. stören. · **to appease:** besänftigen. · **judicious:** klug.

140 **junction:** Eisenbahnknotenpunkt. · **to be wrung with s.th.:** (fig.) von etwas aufgewühlt sein. · **compunction:** Gewissensbisse. · **forlorn:** aussichtslos. · **rails:** Gleise.

**141**

There was an Old Man, who when little
Fell casually into a kettle;
  But, growing too stout,
  He could never get out,
So he passed all his life in that kettle.

**142**

There was an Old Lady of Winchelsea,
Who said, "If you needle or pin shall see,
  On the floor of my room,
  Sweep it up with the broom!" –
That exhaustive Old Lady of Winchelsea!

---

141 **casually:** aus Versehen. · **kettle:** Kessel. · **stout:** korpulent.
142 **Winchelsea:** Gemeinde in East Sussex. · **to sweep s.th. up:** etwas
   aufkehren. · **broom:** Besen. · **exhaustive:** erschöpfend.

### 143

There was a Young Lady of Firle,
Whose hair was addicted to curl;
    It curled up a tree,
    And all over the sea,
That expansive Young Lady of Firle.

### 144

There was an Old Person of Rye,
Who went up to town on a fly;
    But they said, "If you cough,
    You are safe to fall off!
You abstemious Old Person of Rye!"

---

143 **Firle:** Ortschaft in East Sussex. · **to be addicted to do s.th.:** dazu
neigen, etwas zu tun. · **to curl:** sich kräuseln. · **expansive:** (fig.)
expansiv, ausdehnungsfähig.
144 **Rye:** Ortschaft in East Sussex. · **to be safe to do s.th.:** sicherlich
etwas tun. · **abstemious:** bescheiden.

**145**

There was an Old Man of Messina,
Whose daughter was named Opsibeena;
　　She wore a small wig,
　　And rode out on a pig,
To the perfect delight of Messina.

**146**

There is a Young Lady, whose nose,
Continually prospers and grows;
　　When it grew out of sight,
　　She exclaimed in a fright,
"Oh! Farewell to the end of my nose!"

---

145 **wig:** Perücke. · **delight:** Freude, Entzücken.
146 **continually:** ständig. · **to prosper:** gedeihen. · **fright:** Furcht, Ent-
　　setzen. · **farewell:** leb wohl.

**147**

There was an Old Person of Cannes,
Who purchased three fowls and a fan;
   Those she placed on a stool,
   And to make them feel cool
She constantly fanned them at Cannes.


**148**

There was an Old Person of Barnes,
Whose garments were covered with darns;
   But they said, "Without doubt,
   You will soon wear them out,
You luminous Person of Barnes!"

---

147 **to purchase:** kaufen. · **fowl:** Huhn. · **fan:** Fächer. · **stool:** Schemel.

148 **Barnes:** Ort in Surrey. · **garment:** Kleidungsstück. · **darn:** geflickte, gestopfte Stelle. · **to wear s.th. out:** etwas verschleißen. · **luminous:** leuchtend, brillant.

**149**

There was an Old Man of Cashmere,
Whose movements were scroobious and queer;
   Being slender and tall,
   He looked over a wall,
And perceived two fat ducks of Cashmere.

**150**

There was an Old Person of Hove,
Who frequented the depths of a grove;
   Where he studied his books,
   With the wrens and the rooks,
That tranquil Old Person of Hove.

149 **Cashmere:** Kaschmir; Region im nordwestlichen Himalaja.  ·
 **scroobious:** von Lear erfundenes Nonsense-Wort, zusammenge-
setzt aus *scurrilous* ›skurril‹, *curious* ›seltsam‹, *dubious* ›zweifel-
haft‹.  · **queer:** seltsam.  · **slender:** schlank.  · **to perceive:** wahrnehmen.
150 **Hove:** Stadt in East Sussex am Ärmelkanal.  · **to frequent:** besuchen.  · **grove:** Hain.  · **wren:** Zaunkönig.  · **rook:** Saatkrähe.  ·
**tranquil:** ruhig.

**151**

There was an Old Person of Down,
Whose face was adorned with a frown;
   When he opened the door,
   For one minute or more,
He alarmed all the people of Down.

**152**

There was an Old Man of Dunluce,
Who went out to sea on a goose:
   When he'd gone out a mile,
   He observ'd with a smile,
"It is time to return to Dunluce."

---

151 **Down:** nordirische Grafschaft. · **to adorn:** schmücken. · **frown:**
Stirnrunzeln.
152 **Dunluce:** Ort in Nordirland. · **to observe:** bemerken, sagen.

79

### 153

There was a Young Person of Kew,
Whose virtues and vices were few;
   But with blameable haste,
   She devoured some hot paste,
Which destroyed that Young Person of Kew.

### 154

There was an Old Person of Sark,
Who made an unpleasant remark;
   But they said, "Don't you see
   What a brute you must be!
You obnoxious Old Person of Sark."

---

153 **Kew:** Vorort von London. · **virtues and vices:** Tugenden und Laster. · **blameable:** tadelnswert. · **to devour:** verschlingen. · **paste:** Brei.
154 **Sark:** viertgrößte der Kanalinseln. · **brute:** brutaler Kerl. · **obnoxious:** schädlich.

**155**

There was an Old Person of Filey,
Of whom his acquaintance spoke highly;
   He danced perfectly well,
   To the sound of a bell,
And delighted the people of Filey.

**156**

There was an Old Man of El Hums,
Who lived upon nothing but crumbs,
   Which he picked off the ground,
   With the other birds round,
In the roads and the lanes of El Hums.

---

155 **Filey:** Ort in North Yorkshire. · **acquaintance:** Bekanntschaft. ·
**to delight:** erfreuen.
156 **El Hums:** Ort nicht identifizierbar. · **crumb:** Krümel. · **lane:**
Landsträßchen; Gasse.

**157**

There was an Old Man of West Dumpet,
Who possessed a large nose like a trumpet;
   When he blew it aloud,
   It astonished the crowd,
And was heard through the whole of West Dumpet.

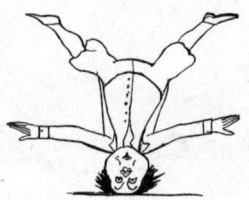

**158**

There was an Old Man of Port Grigor,
Whose actions were noted for vigour;
   He stood on his head,
   Till his waistcoat turned red,
That eclectic Old Man of Port Grigor.

---

157 **West Dumpet:** Ort nicht identifizierbar.
158 **Port Grigor:** Ort nicht identifizierbar. · **vigour:** Kraft. · **waistcoat:** Wams, Weste. · **eclectic:** eklektisch, zusammenstückelnd
(gibt hier keinen Sinn).

**159**

There was an Old Person of Bar,
Who passed all her life in a jar,
   Which she painted pea-green,
   To appear more serene,
That placid Old Person of Bar.

**160**

There was an Old Person of Pett,
Who was partly consumed by regret;
   He sate in a cart,
   And ate cold apple tart,
Which relieved that Old Person of Pett.

---

159 **Bar:** Küstenstadt in Montenegro. · **jar:** Krug. · **serene:** heiter. ·
**placid:** friedlich.
160 **Pett:** Ort in East Sussex. · **to be consumed by s.th.:** von etwas
verzehrt sein. · **regret:** Bedauern. · **sate** (arch.): *sat.* · **to relieve:**
erleichtern.

### 161

There was an Old Person of Newry,
Whose manners were tinctured with fury;
    He tore all the rugs,
    And broke all the jugs
Within twenty miles' distance of Newry.

### 162

There was an Old Person of Jodd,
Whose ways were perplexing and odd;
    She purchased a whistle,
    And sate on a thistle,
And squeaked to the people of Jodd.

---

161 **Newry:** Ort in Nordirland. · **to be tinctured with s.th.:** einen Beigeschmack von etwas haben. · **fury:** Wut. · **rug:** Teppich. · **jug:**
   Krug.
162 **Jodd:** Ort nicht identifizierbar. · **perplexing:** verwirrend. · **odd:**
   seltsam. · **to purchase:** kaufen. · **whistle:** Pfeife (Blasinstrument). · **sate** (arch.): *sat*. · **thistle:** Distel. · **to squeak:** quieken.

**163**

There was an Old Person of Shoreham,
Whose habits were marked by decorum;
    He bought an umbrella,
    And sate in the cellar,
Which pleased all the people of Shoreham.

**164**

There was an Old Man of Dumbree,
Who taught little owls to drink tea;
    For he said, "To eat mice,
    Is not proper or nice,"
That amiable Man of Dumbree.

---

163 **Shoreham:** Ort in Sussex. · **decorum:** Stil, Anstand. · **sate** (arch.): *sat.*
164 **Dumbree:** Ort nicht identifizierbar. · **owl:** Eule. · **amiable:** liebenswürdig.

**165**

There was an Old Person of Wilts,
Who constantly walked upon stilts;
    He wreathed them with lilies,
    And daffy-down-dillies,
That elegant Person of Wilts.

**166**

There was an Old Man whose remorse,
Induced him to drink caper sauce;
    For they said, "If mixed up,
    With some cold claret-cup,
It will certainly soothe your remorse!"

---

165  **Wilts:** Kurzform von *Wiltshire*. • **stilt:** Stelze. • **to wreathe:** bekränzen. • **lily:** Lilie. • **daffy-down-dilly** (poet.): *daffodil:* Narzisse.
166  **remorse:** Gewissen. • **to induce s.o. to do s.th.:** jdn. dazu verleiten, etwas zu tun. • **caper sauce:** Kapernsoße (helle Soße mit Kapern, den in Essig eingelegten Blütenknospen des Kapernstrauchs). • **claret-cup:** Rotweinbowle. • **to soothe:** beruhigen.

**167**

There was an Old Person of Cassel,
Whose nose finished off in a tassel;
    But they call'd out, "Oh well! –
    Don't it look like a bell!"
Which perplexed that Old Person of Cassel.

**168**

There was a Young Person of Janina,
Whose uncle was always a fanning her;
    When he fanned off her head,
    She smiled sweetly, and said,
"You propitious Old Person of Janina!"

167 **Cassel: 1.** Stadt in Nordfrankreich an der Grenze zu Belgien; **2.** alte Schreibung von *Kassel*. · **tassel:** Quaste. · **don't:** *doesn't*; s.
Anm. zu Nr. 11 und vgl. Nr. 15 und 53. · **to perplex:** verwirren,
verblüffen.
168 **Janina:** Stadt in Griechenland. · **a fanning:** *a-fanning* (arch.): *fanning* (*to fan:* fächeln). · **propitious:** wohlgesinnt.

**169**

There was an Old Person of Ware,
Who rode on the back of a bear:
    When they ask'd, –"Does it trot?" –
    He said, "Certainly not!
He's a Moppsikon Floppsikon bear!"


**170**

There was an Old Person of Dean
Who dined on one pea, and one bean;
    For he said, "More than that,
    Would make me too fat,"
That cautious Old Person of Dean.


169 **Ware:** Stadt in Hertfordshire. · **Moppsikon Floppsikon:** Wortschöpfung; Wortspiel mit *mop* ›Mop‹, ›Lappen‹ und *to flop*
›plumpsen‹.
170 **Dean:** *Forest of Dean:* Waldgebiet in Gloucestershire. · **cautious:**
vorsichtig.

**171**

There was an Old Person of Dundalk,
Who tried to teach fishes to walk;
    When they tumbled down dead,
    He grew weary, and said,
"I had better go back to Dundalk!"

**172**

There was a Young Person of Ayr,
Whose head was remarkably square:
    On the top, in fine weather,
    She wore a gold feather;
Which dazzled the people of Ayr.

---

171 **Dundalk:** Stadt in Irland. · **to tumble down:** hinfallen. · **weary:** überdrüssig.
172 **Ayr:** Stadt in Schottland. · **remarkably:** bemerkenswert. · **square:** quadratisch. · **to dazzle:** blenden.

### 173

There was an Old Person of Skye,
Who waltz'd with a bluebottle fly:
    They buzz'd a sweet tune,
    To the light of the moon,
And entranced all the people of Skye.

### 174

There was an Old Man of Dunblane,
Who greatly resembled a crane;
    But they said, – "Is it wrong,
    Since your legs are so long,
To request you won't stay in Dunblane?"

---

173 **Skye:** schottische Insel.  ·  **to waltz:** Walzer tanzen.  ·  **bluebottle fly:** Schmeißfliege.  ·  **to buzz:** summen.  ·  **to entrance:** entzücken.
174 **Dunblane:** Kleinstadt in Schottland.  ·  **to resemble:** ähneln.  ·  **crane:** Kranich.  ·  **to request:** bitten.

### 175

There was an Old Person of Hyde,
Who walked by the shore with his bride,
　　Till a crab who came near,
　　Fill'd their bosoms with fear,
And they said, "Would we'd never left Hyde!"

### 176

There was an Old Person of Rimini,
Who said, "Gracious! Goodness! O Gimini!"
　　When they said, "Please be still!"
　　She ran down a hill,
And was never more heard of at Rimini.

---

175 **Hyde:** Gemeinde in Cheshire. · **crab:** Krabbe. · **bosom:** Brust.
176 **Gracious! / Goodness!:** Du meine Güte! Ach, du liebe Güte! · **O
Gimini!:** Herrje!

### 177

There was an Old Man in a tree,
Whose whiskers were lovely to see;
   But the birds of the air,
   Pluck'd them perfectly bare,
To make themselves nests in that tree.

### 178

There was a Young Lady of Corsica,
Who purchased a little brown saucy-cur;
   Which she fed upon ham,
   And hot raspberry jam,
That expensive Young Lady of Corsica.

---

177 **whiskers** (pl.): Backenbart. · **to pluck s.th. bare:** etwas kahl rupfen, völlig auszupfen.
178 **to purchase:** kaufen. · **saucy-cur:** frecher Köter. · **raspberry jam:** Himbeermarmelade. · **expensive:** hier: spendabel.

**179**

There was an Old Person of Bray,
Who sang through the whole of the day
   To his ducks and his pigs,
   Whom he fed upon figs,
That valuable Person of Bray.


**180**

There was an Old Person of Sestri,
Who sate himself down in the vestry,
   When they said, "You are wrong!" –
   He merely said, "Bong!"
That repulsive Old Person of Sestri.


179 **Bray:** Badeort südlich von Dublin. · **fig:** Feige. · **valuable:** wertvoll.
180 **Sestri:** Ortschaft in der Provinz Genua (Italien). · **sate** (arch.): *sat*. · **vestry:** Sakristei. · **merely:** bloß. · **bong!:** etwa: na und! · **repulsive:** abstoßend, widerlich.

**181**

There was an Old Person of Bude,
Whose deportment was vicious and crude;
   He wore a large ruff,
   Of pale straw-coloured stuff,
Which perplexed all the people of Bude.

**182**

There was an Old Person of Bow,
Whom nobody happened to know;
   So they gave him some soap,
   And said coldly, "We hope
You will go back directly to Bow!"

---

181 **Bude:** Badeort in North Cornwall. · **deportment:** Verhalten, Betragen. · **vicious:** boshaft. · **crude:** grob. · **ruff:** Halskrause. · **stuff:** Zeug; (arch.) Wolle. · **to perplex:** verwirren.
182 **Bow:** Stadtteil von London.

94

**183**

There was a Young Lady of Greenwich,
Whose garments were border'd with spinach;
  But a large spotty calf,
  Bit her shawl quite in half,
Which alarmed that Young Lady of Greenwich.

**184**

There was an Old Person of Brigg,
Who purchased no end of a wig;
  So that only his nose,
  And the end of his toes,
Could be seen when he walked about Brigg.

---

183 **Greenwich:** Vorort von London. · **garments** (pl.): Kleidung. ·
**bordered:** umrandet, eingefasst. · **spinach:** Spinat. · **spotty:** gefleckt. · **shawl:** Umhang.
184 **Brigg:** Ort in North Lincolnshire. · **to purchase:** kaufen. · **no end
of a wig** (infml.): eine Wahnsinns-Perücke, eine riesige Perücke.

**185**

There was an Old Person of Crowle,
Who lived in the nest of an owl;
    When they screamed in the nest,
    He screamed out with the rest,
That depressing Old Person of Crowle.


**186**

There was an Old Person in gray,
Whose feelings were tinged with dismay;
    She purchased two parrots,
    And fed them with carrots,
Which pleased that Old Person in gray.

---

185 **Crowle:** Ortschaft in North Lincolnshire. · **owl:** Eule. · **to scream:**
kreischen. · **depressing:** deprimierend.
186 **to be tinged with s.th.:** nicht frei von etwas sein, eine Spur von etwas haben. · **dismay:** Bestürzung. · **to purchase:** kaufen. · **parrot:** Papagei.

**187**

There was an Old Person of Blythe,
Who cut up his meat with a scythe;
    When they said, "Well! I never!" –
    He cried, "Scythes for ever!"
That lively Old Person of Blythe.

**188**

There was an Old Person of Ealing,
Who was wholly devoid of good feeling;
    He drove a small gig,
    With three owls and a pig,
Which distressed all the people of Ealing.

---

187 **Blythe:** vermutl. *Blythe Bridge:* Ort in Staffordshire. • **scythe:**
Sense. • **lively:** lebhaft, munter.
188 **Ealing:** Vorort von London. • **to be devoid of s.th.:** frei von etwas
sein, etwas nicht haben. • **gig:** zweirädriger Einspänner. • **owl:**
Eule. • **to distress:** bestürzen.

### 189

There was an Old Person of Ickley,
Who could not abide to ride quickly,
    He rode to Karnak,
    On a tortoise's back,
That moony Old Person of Ickley.

### 190

There was an Old Man of Ancona,
Who found a small dog with no owner,
    Which he took up and down,
    All the streets of the town;
That anxious Old Man of Ancona.

---

189 **Ickley:** vermutl. fälschlich für *Ilkley:* Ort in West Yorkshire. · **not to abide to do s.th.:** es nicht ertragen, aushalten, etwas zu tun. · **Karnak:** Dorf in Oberägypten. · **tortoise:** Schildkröte. · **moony:** verträumt.
190 **Ancona:** italienische Hafenstadt an der mittleren Adriaküste. · **anxious:** ängstlich.

**191**

There was an Old Person of Grange,
Whose manners were scroobious and strange;
   He sailed to St. Blubb,
   In a waterproof tub,
That aquatic Old Person of Grange.

**192**

There was an Old Person of Nice,
Whose associates were usually geese.
   They walked out together,
   In all sorts of weather;
That affable Person of Nice!

---

191 **Grange:** Ort nicht identifizierbar.  · **scroobious:** Wortschöpfung;
  vgl. Nr. 39.  · **St. Blubb:** Ort nicht identifizierbar.  · **tub:** Wanne.  ·
  **aquatic:** auf dem Wasser lebend.
192 **Nice:** Nizza.  · **associate:** Partner.  · **affable:** freundlich.

**193**

There was an Old Person of Deal
Who in walking, used only his heel;
   When they said, "Tell us why?" –
   He made no reply;
That mysterious Old Person of Deal.

**194**

There was an Old Man of Thermopylae,
Who never did anything properly;
   But they said, "If you choose,
   To boil eggs in your shoes,
You shall never remain in Thermopylae."

193 **Deal:** Stadt in Kent. · **heel:** Ferse. · **mysterious:** rätselhaft; ge-
heimnisvoll.
194 **Thermopylae** (pl.): die Thermopylen; Engstelle in Mittelgriechen-
land, in der Antike von hohem strategischem Wert.

### 195

There was an Old Person of Minety
Who purchased five hundred and ninety
   Large apples and pears,
   Which he threw unawares,
At the heads of the people of Minety.

### 196

There was an Old Man whose despair
Induced him to purchase a hare:
   Whereon one fine day,
   He rode wholly away,
Which partly assuaged his despair.

---

195 **Minety:** Ort in Wiltshire. · **to purchase:** kaufen. · **unawares** (adv.): unerwartet, unvermutet.
196 **despair:** Verzweiflung. · **to induce s.o. to do s.th.:** jdn. veranlassen, etwas zu tun. · **to purchase:** kaufen. · **hare:** Hase. · **to assuage:** mildern.

**197**

There was an Old Person of Pinner,
As thin as a lath, if not thinner;
    They dressed him in white,
    And roll'd him up tight,
That elastic Old Person of Pinner.

**198**

There was an Old Person of Bromley,
Whose ways were not cheerful or comely;
    He sate in the dust,
    Eating spiders and crust,
That unpleasing Old Person of Bromley.

---

197 **Pinner:** Vorort von London. · **lath:** Latte.
198 **Bromley:** Name mehrerer Orte in England. · **cheerful:** fröhlich. ·
**comely:** etwa: gesittet. · **sate** (arch.): *sat*. · **crust:** (Brot-)Kruste,
Rinde.

### 199

There was an Old Man of Dunrose;
A parrot seized hold of his nose.
    When he grew melancholy,
    They said, "His name's Polly,"
Which soothed that Old Man of Dunrose.

### 200

There was an Old Man on the Border,
Who lived in the utmost disorder;
    He danced with the cat,
    And made tea in his hat,
Which vexed all the folks on the Border.

---

199 **Dunrose:** Ort nicht identifizierbar. • **parrot:** Papagei. • **to seize hold of s.th.:** etwas fest packen. • **to soothe:** beruhigen.
200 **Border:** Grenzgebiet zwischen England und Schottland (*border:* Grenze). • **utmost:** äußerste(r, s). • **disorder:** Durcheinander. • **to vex:** irritieren. • **folks:** Leute.

**201**

There was an Old Man of Spithead,
Who opened the window, and said, –
  "Fil-jomble, fil-jumble,
  Fil-rumble-come-tumble!"
That doubtful Old Man of Spithead.

**202**

There was an Old Person of Sheen,
Whose expression was calm and serene;
  He sate in the water,
  And drank bottled porter,
That placid Old Person of Sheen.

---

201 **Spithead:** Teil einer Meerenge in Hampshire. · **doubtful:** zweifelnd, ungläubig, skeptisch.
202 **Sheen:** *East Sheen:* Vorort von London. · **serene:** heiter. · **sate** (arch.): *sat.* · **porter:** Biersorte. · **placid:** friedlich.

**203**

There was an Old Person of Florence,
Who held mutton chops in abhorrence;
　　He purchased a bustard,
　　And fried him in mustard,
Which choked that Old Person of Florence.

**204**

There was an Old Person of Loo,
Who said, "What on earth shall I do?"
　　When they said, "Go away!" –
　　She continued to stay,
That vexatious Old Person of Loo.

---

203 **to hold s.th. in abhorrence:** Abscheu vor etwas haben. · **mutton chop:** Hammelkotelett. · **to purchase:** kaufen. · **bustard:** Trappe (dem Kranich verwandter großer brauner Vogel). · **mustard:** Senf. · **to choke:** ersticken.
204 **Loo:** Name mehrerer Orte in den Niederlanden. · **vexatious:** lästig.

**205**

There was an Old Person of Pisa,
Whose daughters did nothing to please her;
   She dressed them in gray,
   And banged them all day,
Round the walls of the city of Pisa.

**206**

There was an Old Man in a garden,
Who always begged every-one's pardon;
   When they asked him, "What for?" –
   He replied, "You're a bore!
And I trust you'll go out of my garden."

205 **to bang:** schlagen.
206 **bore:** Langweiler.

**207**

There was an Old Man of Thames Ditton,
Who called for something to sit on;
    But they brought him a hat,
    And said – "Sit upon that,
You abruptious Old Man of Thames Ditton!"

**208**

There was an Old Man of Dee-side
Whose hat was exceedingly wide,
    But he said, "Do not fail,
    If it happen to hail
To come under my hat at Dee-side!"

---

207 **Thames Ditton:** Ortschaft in Surrey. · **abruptious:** Lears Variante
von *abrupt* ›plötzlich‹, ›schroff‹.
208 **Dee-side:** Ufer des (schottischen oder walisischen) Flusses Dee. ·
**exceedingly:** äußerst. · **to fail:** versäumen. · **to hail:** hageln.

**209**

There was an Old Man at a station,
Who made a promiscuous oration;
   But they said, "Take some snuff! –
   You have talk'd quite enough
You afflicting Old Man at a station!"

**210**

There was an Old Person of Shields,
Who frequented the valley and fields;
   All the mice and the cats,
   And the snakes and the rats,
Followed after that Person of Shields.

---

209 **promiscuous:** hier etwa: wirr. · **oration:** Rede. · **snuff:** Schnupfta-
bak. · **afflicting:** etwa: anstrengend.
210 **Shields:** englische Hafenstadt. · **to frequent:** häufig aufsuchen.

**211**

There was a Young Person in pink,
Who called out for something to drink;
   But they said, "O my daughter,
    There's nothing but water!"
Which vexed that Young Person in pink.


**212**

There was a Young Person whose history,
Was always considered a mystery;
   She sate in a ditch,
    Although no one knew which,
And composed a small treatise on history.


211 **to vex:** irritieren, ärgern.
212 **sate** (arch.): *sat.* · **ditch:** Graben. · **treatise:** Abhandlung.

**213**

There was an old sailor of Compton,
Whose vessel a rock it once bump'd on,
   The shock was so great,
   That it damaged the pate,
Of that singular sailor of Compton.

**214**

There was an Old Man of New York,
Who murdered himself with a fork;
   But nobody cried,
   Though he very soon died,
For that silly Old Man of New York.

213 **Compton:** Name mehrerer Orte in England. · **vessel:** Schiff. · **rock:** Felsen. · **to bump on s.th.:** auf etwas auflaufen. · **pate** (slang): Rübe (Kopf). · **singular:** einmalig.

110

**215**

There was an Old Man of Kildare,
Who climbed into a very high chair;
　　When he said, – "Here I stays,
　　Till the end of my days,"
That immovable Man of Kildare.

215 **Kildare:** Grafschaft in der Republik Irland. · **I stays:** *I stay*; s.
Anm. zu Nr. 11 und vgl. Nr. 15, 53 und 167. · **immovable: 1.** unbe-
weglich, bewegungslos; **2.** (fig.) unerschütterlich.

# Editorische Notiz

Das vorliegende Bändchen enthält alle 216 zu Lears Lebzeiten veröffentlichten Limericks. Der Text folgt den Ausgaben: *The Complete Nonsense of Edward Lear*, hrsg. und mit einer Einleitung von Holbrook Jackson, London: Faber and Faber, 1947 (Nr. 1–212) und *Edward Lear: The Complete Nonsense and Verse*, hrsg. von Vivien Noakes, London: Penguin, 2006 (Nr. 213–215).

Das Glossar enthält in der Regel alle Wörter, die im *Thematischen Grund- und Aufbauwortschatz Englisch* von Gernot Häublein und Recs Jenkins (Stuttgart/Düsseldorf/Leipzig: Ernst Klett Verlag, 1993) nicht zum Grundwortschatz gehören.

*Im Glossar verwendete englische Abkürzungen*

| | |
|---|---|
| adv. | adverb |
| arch. | archaic (veraltet) |
| fig. | figuratively (übertragen) |
| hum. | humorously |
| infml. | informal (umgangssprachlich) |
| o.s. | oneself |
| pl. | plural |
| poet. | poetical (dichterisch, gehoben) |
| s.o. | someone |
| s.th. | something |

# Literaturhinweise

## 1. Ausgaben

*A Book of Nonsense*, by Derry down Derry, London 1846.

*Nonsense Songs, Stories, Botany, and Alphabets*, London 1871.

*More Nonsense, Pictures, Rhymes, Botany, etc*, London 1872.

*Laughable Lyrics*, London 1877.

*The Complete Nonsense of Edward Lear*, hrsg. von H. Jackson, London 1947 [u. ö.].

*Letters of Edward Lear, Author of The Book of Nonsense, to Chichester Fortescue, Lord Carlingford, and Frances Countess Waldgrave*, hrsg. von Lady Strachey, Freeport 1970.

*Lear in the Original*, hrsg. von H. W. Liebert, New York 1975.

*Edward Lear: A Book of Bosh*, hrsg. von B. Alderson, Harmondsworth 1975 [u. ö.].

*Nonsensus*, hrsg. von J. G. Schiller, Stroud 1988.

*Selected Letters*, hrsg. von V. Noakes, Oxford 1990.

*Book of Nonsense and Nonsense Songs*, Claremont 1996.

*Selected Poems of Edward Lear*, hrsg. von G. Herbert und I. Hamilton, London 1997.

*Edward Lear: The Complete Nonsense and Verse*, hrsg. von V. Noakes, London 2006.

## 2. Deutsche Übersetzungen

H. C. Artmann, *Edward Lears Nonsense-Verse*, Frankfurt a. M. 1964.

G. Fischer, *Wie nett, Herrn Lear zu kennen*, München 1965.

H. A. Halbey, *Der Quingelwingelquie*, Bilder von H. Oxenbury, Freising 1969 [u. ö.].

U. Friesel, *Die Geschichte der sieben Familien vom Pippel-Poppel-See*, München 1973.

J. Guggenmos, *Phantastische Reise. Nonsensgedichte*, Weinheim 1973.

J. Guggenmos, *Von Eule und Katz und anderm Geschwatz*, Frankfurt a. M. 1979.

H. M. Enzensberger, *Edward Lears kompletter Nonsens*, 2 Bde., Frankfurt a. M. 1980.

– *Die Ente und das Känguruh und andere Gedichte*, Wien 1992.

V. Pohl, *Die Geschichte von den vier kleinen Kindern, die rund um die Welt zogen*, Berlin 1992.

## 3. Sekundärliteratur

### a) Zu Edward Lear allgemein

A. Davidson, *Edward Lear: Landscape Painter and Nonsense Poet (1812–1888)*, London 1938; Nachdr. 1968.

V. Noakes, *Edward Lear: The Life of a Wanderer*, London 1968; rev. Ausg. Stroud 2004.

J. Lehmann, *Edward Lear and his World*, London 1977.

V. Noakes, *Edward Lear, 1812–1888*, London 1985 / New York 1986.

S. Chitty, *That Singular Person Called Lear: A Biography*, London 1988.

G. Kamen, *Edward Lear, King of Nonsense: A Biography*, New York 1990.

A. Barry, »Edward Lear«, in: *Book and Magazine Collector* 88 (1991) S. 22–29.

P. Levi, *Edward Lear: A Biography*, London 1995.

### b) Lear als Zeichner und Maler

B. Reade, *Edward Lear's Parrots*, London 1949.

P. Hofer, *Edward Lear as a Landscape Draughtsman*, Cambridge (Mass.) 1967.

A. Thorpe, *The Birds of Edward Lear*, London 1975.

S. Hyman, *Edward Lear's Birds*, London 1980.

E. Lear, *The Parrots*, Köln 2009.

c) Lear als Autor

T. Byrom, *Nonsense and Wonder: The Poems and Cartoons of Edward Lear*, New York 1977.

A.K. Lyons [u.a.], *A Concordance to the Complete Nonsense of Edward Lear*, Norwood (Pa.) 1980.

I.R. Hark, *Edward Lear*, Boston 1982.

A.C. Colley, »Edward Lear's Limericks and the Reversals of Nonsense«, in: *Victorian Poetry* 26 (1988) S. 285–299.

Th. Stemmler, »Die Last der Heuschrecke – Edward Lear«, in: *Frankfurter Allgemeine Zeitung Magazin* 413 (1988) S. 38–41.

A.C. Colley, »Edward Lear's Anti-Colonial Bestiary«, in: *Victorian Poetry* 30 (1992) S. 109–120.

– Edward Lear and the Critics, Columbia 1993.

Th. Dilworth, »Society and the Self in the Limericks of Lear«, in: *Review of English Studies* 45 (1994) S. 42–62.

– »Edward Lear's Suicide Limerick«, in: *Review of English Studies* 46 (1995) S. 535–538.

Th. Stemmler, »Edward Lears Zoo«, in: *Sinn im Unsinn. Über Unsinnsdichtung vom Mittelalter bis zum 20. Jahrhundert*, hrsg. von Th. Stemmler und St. Horlacher, Tübingen 1997, S. 71–86.

J. Rieder, »Edward Lear's Limericks: The Function of Children's Nonsense Poetry«, in: *Children's Literature* 26 (1998) S. 47–60.

Th. Stemmler, »Sie spielten verrückt und lachten entzückt. Der große Dichter des Nonsens: Applaus für Edward Lear …«, in: *Frankfurter Allgemeine Zeitung* 109 (12.5.2005) S. 40.

d) Zum Limerick und zur Nonsense-Literatur

H.L. Reed, *The Complete Limerick Book*, London 1924.

E. Sewell, *The Field of Nonsense*, London 1952.

G. Legman, *The Limerick: 1700 Examples [...]*, Paris 1953; London 1974.

A. Liede, *Dichtung als Spiel. Studien zur Unsinnspoesie an den Grenzen der Sprache*, 2 Bde., Berlin 1963.

W. S. Baring-Gould, *The Lure of the Limerick*, London 1968.

R. Hildebrandt, *Nonsense-Aspekte der englischen Kinderliteratur*, Weinheim 1970.

A. Schöne, *Englische Nonsense- und Grusel-Balladen*, Göttingen 1970.

D. Petzold, *Formen und Funktionen der englischen Nonsense-Dichtung im 19. Jahrhundert*, Nürnberg 1972.

K. Reichert, *Lewis Carroll. Studien zum literarischen Unsinn*, München 1974.

J. Harrowven, *The Limerick Makers*, London 1976.

C. W. Thomsen, *Das Groteske und die englische Literatur*, Darmstadt 1977.

C. Bibby, *The Art of the Limerick*, London 1978.

W. Tigges (Hrsg.), *Explorations in the Field of Nonsense*, Amsterdam 1987.

A. Caboni, *Nonsense: Edward Lear e la tradizione del nonsense inglese*, Rom 1988.

A. C. Colley, »The Limerick and the Space of Metaphor«, in: *Genre* 21 (1988) S. 65–91.

W. Tigges, *An Anatomy of Literary Nonsense*, Amsterdam 1988.

P. Köhler, *Nonsens. Theorie und Geschichte der literarischen Gattung*, Heidelberg 1989.

– (Hrsg.), *Das Nonsens-Buch*, Stuttgart 1990.

J.-J. Lecercle, *Philosophy of Nonsense: The Intuitions of Victorian Nonsense Literature*, London 1994.

E. Rossiter, *A Theory of Nonsense*, Diss. University of Westminster 1996 [unveröff.].

N. Malcolm, *The Origins of English Nonsense*, London 1997.

Th. Stemmler / St. Horlacher (Hrsg.), *Sinn im Unsinn. Über Unsinnsdichtung vom Mittelalter bis zum 20. Jahrhundert*, Tübingen 1997.

W. Raveling (Hrsg.), *Limericks*, Stuttgart 1999.

# Nachwort

## Dämonen

Hinter dem Wort »Demon« verbarg Lear vor den Zeitgenossen mit Erfolg seine Epilepsie, an der er seit frühester Kindheit litt – wohl seit seinem fünften oder sechsten Lebensjahr. Doch damit nicht genug: Noch weit mehr belastete bereits den jungen Lear. Asthma, Bronchitis, Kurzsichtigkeit plagten ihn, und seit seinem siebten Lebensjahr suchten ihn weitere Dämonen heim: von ihm verhüllend »Morbids« genannte schwere Depressionen. Dazu war er nicht gerade ein Adonis. Vielleicht hat er sich hässlicher gemacht, als er es in Wirklichkeit war, doch in seinem autobiographischen Gedicht *How pleasant to know Mr. Lear* zieht er gnadenlos über sich her:

> His mind is concrete and fastidious,
>     His nose is remarkably big;
> His visage is more or less hideous,
>     His beard it resembles a wig.

(Sein Geist ist konkret und anspruchsvoll, / seine Nase ist bemerkenswert groß; / sein Gesicht ist mehr oder weniger scheußlich, / sein Bart ähnelt einer Perücke.)

Solch ein mehrfach behinderter Mensch bedarf angestrengter Liebe. Diese hat ihm seine Mutter kaum geben können: Er durfte als zwanzigstes von einundzwanzig Kindern konzentrierte Zuneigung nicht erwarten. Die wurde ihm paradoxerweise erst zuteil, als die Familie durch den Bankrott des Vaters, der Börsenmakler war, auseinanderbrach.

Edward wurde nunmehr (seit 1816) von seiner ältesten Schwester Ann erzogen: der Vierjährige (1812 geboren) von der Fünfundzwanzigjährigen (1791 geboren). Lange Jahre in den Händen einer fürsorglichen, wesentlich älteren Schwester – dies hinterlässt Spuren. Obwohl ihr Lear viel – auch

Zeichenunterricht – zu verdanken hat, äußerte er sich später nicht immer begeistert über seine Erziehung, an der bis 1822 auch seine Schwester Sarah mitwirkte: »Brought up by women – and badly besides – and ill always […]« (»Von Frauen erzogen – schlecht im Übrigen – und immer krank […]«).

Ein mit so vielen Problemen beladener Mensch kann doch nur melancholisch sein? Weit gefehlt. In Lears Werken – fast allen Texten und einigen Bildern – sind Trauer und Fröhlichkeit auf skurrile Weise kombiniert. Mit dem Mut des Verzweifelten, des Galgenhumoristen, schreibt und zeichnet Lear Komisches. Für ihn gilt Beaumarchais' Wort aus dem *Barbier von Sevilla:* »Ich lache über alles, um nicht darüber weinen zu müssen.« Ein benevolenter Humorist war Lear nicht: Zu oft sind seine Verse bitter und makaber, zu oft grausame *sick jokes.*

## Musen

Wie Goethe, Hoffmann und Barlach war Edward Lear vielbegabt: Zeichner, Maler, Dichter, Komponist. Bereits als Fünfzehnjähriger verdient er erstes Geld mit Zeichnungen von Kranken; diese pathologischen Schaubilder verkauft er an Ärzte und Hospitäler. Bald beginnt er mit dem Zeichnen von Vögeln und bringt es auf diesem Gebiet als Autodidakt zur Meisterschaft – einem Audubon ebenbürtig. Lears lebensechte Papageien-Darstellungen gewinnen die Aufmerksamkeit Lord Stanleys, des späteren 13. Earl of Derby – seinerzeit Präsident der Zoologischen Gesellschaft in London.

Dieser lädt Lear ein, auf seinem Landsitz in Knowsley bei Liverpool Tiere seiner privaten Menagerie zu zeichnen. Dort arbeitet Lear (mit Unterbrechungen) von 1831 bis 1837, dort verfasst er auch für die Kinder der Familie die ersten Nonsense-Verse, die bald auch von den Erwachsenen des Hauses geschätzt werden.

In den folgenden Jahren – bis zu seinem Lebensende –

wohnt Lear an verschiedenen Orten Südeuropas: Rom, Korfu, San Remo; England besucht er immer wieder (etwa zwanzigmal). Ortsfest wird er jedoch nie. Auf der Suche nach immer neuen Motiven für seine Bilder bricht er fast jedes Jahr zu Reisen auf, die ihn nach Griechenland, Palästina, Ägypten, in die Türkei und sogar bis Indien und Ceylon führen. Es ist bewundernswert, welche Strapazen dieser mit vielen Krankheiten Geschlagene auf sich nimmt und meistert; mehrfach entgehen er und sein treuer Diener Giorgio Kokali nur knapp dem Tode.

Als Ausbeute dieser Reisen brachte Lear zahlreiche kolorierte Landschafts-Skizzen »nach Hause« – wo immer dies sein mochte. Dort vollendete er zahlreiche dieser Aquarell-Studien oder benutzte sie als Vorlagen für große Ölbilder. Wenn er in Geldnot war, produzierte er auch Aquarelle im Fließbandverfahren – bis zu 60 in einer Serie. Bewundernswert der Fleiß Lears: Insgesamt hat er etwa 9000 Aquarelle und 300 Ölbilder gemalt.

Daneben fand Lear stets Zeit zum Schreiben – auch während seiner Reisen. Er verfasste mehrere illustrierte Reisebücher, in denen er anschaulich und witzig über seine Erlebnisse berichtet und dem Leser durch seine Zeichnungen ferne Landschaften nahebringt.

Während Nonsense-Elemente in diesen Texten und seinen – nur zum Teil erhaltenen – Tagebüchern eine geringe Rolle spielen, sind sie in seinen Tausenden von Briefen häufig anzutreffen. Auch Lears privateste Äußerungen sind von einer absurden Grundstimmung durchzogen. Seine von Anfang an vielfach gefährdete Existenz führt ihn dazu, ohne Unterlass zu fragen und alles in Frage zu stellen. Durch groteskes Sprach- und Gedankenspiel macht er vermeintlich Sicheres fragwürdig.

Diese methodische Verunsicherung macht vor nichts und niemandem halt: nicht vor seiner eigenen Identität, seiner Malerei, seinen Reisen, Kochrezepten und Balladen. Er nennt sich »Lyar«, »Adopty Duncle«, »Oduardo«, »Arly«, »Derry down Derry«. Noch heute wird zuweilen seine absurde ge-

119

nealogische Behauptung ernst genommen, sein Großvater sei
dänischer Abstammung und habe ursprünglich Lør geheißen.
Er zeichnet sich selbst als Insekt oder Vogel.

Dieses Aufbegehren gegen gesellschaftliche, gedankliche
und sprachliche Normen findet sich konzentriert in seinen
Gedichten – seinem *nonsense verse*. Dort stoßen skurrilen
Wesen mit seltsamen Namen an fantastischen Orten merk-
würdige Dinge zu. Da gibt es einen menschenfressenden
Kummerbund; einen Mr. Discobbolos, der sich und seine Familie in die Luft sprengt; einen Pobble ohne Zehen; einen
Mr. Yonghy-Bonghy-Bò, der um die Hand der Lady Jingly
anhält; und in der Grombulischen Ebene lebt der Dong mit
der Leuchtnase. Der Eindruck, den zahlreiche dieser Gedichte und Lieder hinterlassen, ist zwiespältig – ja paradox. Sie
sind zugleich komisch und tragisch, gefühlvoll und grausam,
irrational und schlüssig – und darin den früher entstandenen
Limericks Edward Lears ähnlich.


## Limericks

Etwa vierzig Jahre lang hat Lear immer wieder Limericks ge-
schrieben – von seiner Zeit in Knowsley Hall (ab 1831) bis
zur Veröffentlichung seines *More Nonsense, Pictures, Rhymes,
Botany, etc.* (1872).

Eine erste Sammlung erschien 1846 unter dem Titel *A
Book of Nonsense*. Sie enthielt 73 Limericks, die – bis auf den
Titel-Limerick – jeweils in drei Zeilen angeordnet waren.
Diese erste (und auch die zweite) Auflage gab als Verfasser
»Derry down Derry« an – Lears Pseudonym. 1855 erschien
eine zweite, inhaltlich unveränderte Auflage; in dieser sind
die Limericks fünfzeilig abgedruckt. Erst die dritte Auflage
des Jahres 1861 wurde ein Erfolg und verhalf der seltsamen
Gedichtgattung des Limericks zu allgemeiner Popularität. Sie
enthielt 70 von den 73 Limericks der Erstausgabe: *The Old
Sailor of Compton, The Old Man of Kildare* und *The Old
Man of New York* wurden – warum auch immer – von Lear

nicht mehr in der Sammlung belassen, dafür 43 neue Limericks aufgenommen. Erstmals gab er sich als Verfasser zu erkennen. Zu seinen Lebzeiten erschienen 24 Auflagen des Buches. Doch der literarische Ruhm brachte Lear geringen finanziellen Gewinn: Er verkaufte 1862 das Copyright für 125 £ an den Verleger Routledge, der ihn unter – gar nicht sanften – Druck gesetzt hatte.

Im folgenden Jahrzehnt schrieb Lear neben einigen Nonsense-Gedichten, -Liedern und -Alphabeten zahlreiche neue Limericks. Einige dieser Texte, jedoch keine Limericks, sammelte er in einem Band *Nonsense Songs, Stories, Botany and Alphabets*, der 1871 erschien. Erst die 1872 erschienene Sammlung *More Nonsense, Pictures, Rhymes, Botany, etc.* (und nur noch diese) enthielt neue Limericks aus der Feder Lears – immerhin hundert. Danach veröffentlichte er keinen einzigen dieser »nonsenses« oder »absurdities« mehr, wie er sie nannte: Das Wort Limerick hat Lear nie verwendet.

Über die Herkunft dieser Bezeichnung ist viel spekuliert worden – mit mäßigem Erfolg. Einige Forscher behaupten einen Zusammenhang mit der irischen Stadt Limerick und eine starke Tradition solcher Texte in Irland, andere haben französische Ursprünge entdeckt, die angeblich durch irische Legionäre nach Irland gebracht worden sind – und andere wiederum leugnen die formale Identität des Wortes mit der gleichnamigen Stadt. Wie dem auch sei – das *Oxford English Dictionary* gibt als Erstbeleg für »limerick« einen Text aus dem Jahre 1896 an und definiert Limericks als »a form of nonsense verse«.

Dieser Begriff bietet nicht nur etymologische, sondern auch semantische und gattungshistorische Probleme. Der Lexikograph Murray hatte 1898 Limericks als »indecent nonsense verse« definiert und damit einen beträchtlichen Teil dieser Gattung richtig charakterisiert, doch nicht alle deren Vertreter. In der Tat sind die meisten Limericks dieser Zeit leicht bis grob pornographisch, während die älteren – insbesondere die Edward Lears – völlig frei von solchen Zügen sind. Der Begriff »Limerick« wird unzulässigerweise verengt gebraucht. Man sollte an der Definition des *Oxford English Dictionary* festhalten, diese jedoch um eine formale Beschreibung erweitern: Limericks sind fünfzeilige Nonsense-Gedichte mit dem Reimmuster *aabba*. Auch wenn Limericks zuweilen drei- oder vierzeilig angeordnet werden – ihre formale Struktur ist die eines Fünfzeilers.

Zu Anfang des 19. Jahrhunderts entsteht auf der formalen Basis ähnlicher Vorläufer der Limerick, wie wir ihn verstehen und oben definiert haben: Nunmehr wird der Fünfzeiler für Nonsense-Themen verwendet. Bereits im Titel der ersten erhaltenen Limerick-Sammlung aus dem Jahre 1820/21 wird die Wichtigkeit des Absurden und Grotesken betont: *The History of Sixteen Wonderful Old Women [...] Exhibiting their Principal Eccentricities and Amusements.* Hier geht es – wie später bei Lear – um Exzentriker.

Lear übernahm zwar die formalen Elemente und den Nonsense dieser frühesten Limericks, ersetzte aber deren harmlose Geschichten durch oft makabre *sick jokes.* Er schmuggelt tieferen Sinn in seinen Un-Sinn ein und berührt Themen, die bis heute nichts von ihrer Aktualität eingebüßt haben.

Zum einen geht es in seinen Limericks – ganz wie in Lears eigenem Leben – um einsame Individuen in der Konfrontation mit der Gesellschaft. Diese Einzelgänger werden wegen ihres unkonventionellen Verhaltens von der verständnislosen Mehrheit verachtet oder gar mitleidlos bekämpft und eliminiert. Seine Nonsense-Geschichten erzählt Lear nicht *just for fun*, sondern um milden Protest anzumelden – Protest gegen das viktorianische Korsett, das alle Lebensbereiche einengte.

Typisch für die frühen Limericks ist ferner die Illustrierung: Ähnlich wie Embleme der Barockzeit wirken sie durch die Einheit von Text und Bild. Und ein weiteres wesentliches Merkmal des »klassischen« Limericks wird in den Titeln der ersten Sammlungen erwähnt: Es wird eine Geschichte erzählt. In dem eben erwähnten Titel ist von »history« die Rede, in den *Anecdotes and Adventures of Fifteen Gentlemen* (1822) von Abenteuern.

Lear hat diese beiden Sammlungen gekannt und sich von

ihnen inspirieren lassen: Er ist eben *nicht*, wie manche behaupten, der Erfinder des Limericks oder gar der Nonsense-Dichtung, allerdings deren wichtigster Repräsentant. Aus der oben erwähnten ersten Sammlung hat er zumindest Text und Zeichnung des ersten und fünften Limericks verwendet. Zu einigen Limericks der zweiten Sammlung hat Lear eigene Zeichnungen angefertigt – so zu dem bekannten *There was a sick man of Tobago*. Diesen Limerick benennt Lear später im Vorwort zu seinem *More Nonsense* (1872) als Quelle seiner Inspiration.

Angesichts dieser historischen Abhängigkeiten liegt die Frage nahe, ob Lears Limericks durch Besonderheiten charakterisiert sind, die sich sonst in der Gattung nicht finden.

In formaler Hinsicht folgen alle Limericks Lears einem gemeinsamen Muster, das bereits vor ihm ausgeprägt war: Hier gibt es nichts Besonderes. Die Limericks bestehen aus fünf Zeilen, die nach dem Schema *aabba* reimen. Das verwendete Metrum ist anapästisch-daktylisch; die *a*-Verse enthalten drei, die *b*-Verse zwei Hebungen. Die bereits in Lears Vorbildern häufige Eingangsformel »There was …« wird bei ihm zur Regel (bis auf eine einzige Ausnahme: Nr. 146). Das erste Reimwort ist meistens, doch nicht immer, ein geographischer Begriff – auch dieses Merkmal fand Lear in den älteren Sammlungen. Bis auf wenige Ausnahmen wird das Reimwort der ersten Zeile als das der letzten wiederholt.

Auch die inhaltliche Struktur folgt älteren Mustern. In der ersten (und oft auch in der zweiten) Zeile wird eine Person dargestellt, in den folgenden drei oder zwei Zeilen meist ein Vorfall beschrieben. Die letzte Zeile hat fast den Charakter eines Refrains: Sie ist in ihrer zweiten Hälfte meist mit der ersten Zeile identisch; in der ersten Hälfte wird das einleitende »There was …« ausgetauscht – oft durch eine adjektivische Charakterisierung der Person. Dieses Adjektiv ist entweder treffend – oder bewusst falsch. In solch absurder Funktion verwendet Lear oft *hard words* (»schwierige Wörter«) wie »abstemious« oder »intrinsic«: So etwas findet sich vor Lear nicht.

Was ist das besonders Wichtige an Lears Limericks? Sie sind persönlich – und damit abgründig. Diese Dimension wird häufig übersehen. Lears Limericks werden oft als harmlose Unterhaltung für Kinder hingestellt. Zu solcher Banalisierung tragen im deutschen Sprachbereich verharmlosende Übersetzungen maßgeblich bei.

In Lears Limericks – Texten und Zeichnungen – lassen sich zahlreiche autobiographische Züge nachweisen. Seine physischen Merkmale tauchen hier grotesk übertrieben wieder auf: gewaltiger Bart, große Nase, dünne Beine, rundlicher Körper. Kindheitserinnerungen an die Großfamilie finden sich ebenso wieder wie seine Angst vor Hunden, extreme Unruhe und Vogelliebe. Vor allem aber sind Lears Limericks Zeugnisse seiner Einsamkeit. In immer wieder neuen Variationen thematisieren sie die Isoliertheit des Aufmüpfigen – des Ex-Zentrikers, der von der Gesellschaft an den Rand gedrängt wird.

Diese Unbotmäßigkeit äußert sich in vielen Erscheinungsformen: in ungewöhnlicher Kleidung, merkwürdigen Essgewohnheiten und seltsamen Aktivitäten. Lears Gestalten klettern auf Bäume, schlafen auf Tischen, tanzen mit Tieren, sind ständig auf Reisen – und auf der Flucht. Oft schreien sie verzweifelt und versuchen Kontakt mit den anderen zu finden. Diese anderen, die anonymen, angepassten Massen, stehen dem Nichtangepassten häufig feindselig gegenüber; bisweilen erschlagen sie ihn sogar. Die Verzweiflung und Depressionen des Einzelgängers werden ausdrücklich benannt (z. B. in Nr. 57 oder 91) oder kaum verhüllt beschrieben (z. B. in Nr. 113). In seiner lyrischen Verdichtung macht uns ein Limerick (Nr. 92) besonders betroffen:

There was an Old Man who said, »Well!
Will *nobody* answer this bell?
  I have pulled day and night,
  Till my hair has grown white,
But nobody answers this bell!«

Lears Zeichnung zeigt einen Mann, der verzweifelt an einem Glockenseil zieht und um Einlass – gesellschaftliche Zulassung – bittet. Dies hat er, wie er sagt, sein ganzes Leben lang versucht – vergeblich.

## Lears Zoo

Kein Wunder, dass ein einsamer Mensch wie Edward Lear, der weder bei Männern noch Frauen (einen Mann hätte er bevorzugt) erotischen Erfolg hatte, Zuflucht bei Tieren suchte. Auch seinen Figuren in den Limericks werden die Tiere zu Vorbildern, Freunden und Leidensgefährten. Kein Schriftsteller hat Tiere so ernst genommen wie Edward Lear. Nicht nur in seinen Limericks wimmelt es von unseren Mitgeschöpfen, gleich welcher zoologischen Gattung oder Art sie zugehören.

Mehr noch: In Lears Werken kommt die Welt der Tiere der des Menschen sehr nahe. Die Tiere erhalten menschliche Züge, die Tiere menschliche. Lears Zeichnung zu Limerick Nr. 80 illustriert diese Grenzüberschreitung vortrefflich:

Hier wird der Sinn im Unsinn greifbar – begreifbar. Kein Vogel sieht so aus, kein Mensch trägt solche Züge. Menschenvogel und Vogelmensch begegnen sich: Gleich groß und gleich wichtig stehen sie sich gegenüber.

Die frei schwimmenden und fliegenden Tiere liegen Lear besonders am Herzen, und die freiesten aller freien – die Vögel – ganz besonders: Sie stellen ein Drittel aller Passagiere in der Arche des Dichters. Und wie benehmen sich diese Reisegefährten? Meistens sehr manierlich. Nur ab und zu fällt eines der Tiere aus der Rolle: Dann bedroht es den Menschen oder schadet ihm gar. In derartigen Fällen folgt das Tier seiner Natur – und nicht dem visionären, doch leider unsinnigen Diktat des Dichters. So gibt es in den Limericks auch gefräßige Ratten (27), einen menschenfressenden Hund (75) und so weiter.

In den allermeisten Limericks ist das Verhältnis zwischen Mensch und Tier ungetrübt. Diese kreatürliche Gemeinsamkeit spiegelt sich bildlich in mancher Metamorphose wider. Der oben angeführten (80) kann man weitere hinzufügen. Da wird etwa (in 119) der Mensch zum Fisch oder (in 10) eine Biene zum Pfeifenraucher. In vielen Limericks frönen Mensch und Tier gemeinsam der Unterhaltung durch Tanz und Musik. So tanzt ein älterer Herr mit einer Fliege (173), mit einer Katze (200) oder einem Raben (74). Dass solcher Umgang mit Tieren nicht den Beifall aller Menschen findet, ist zu erwarten. Diese bornierten »anderen« – »they« nennt sie Lear – schrecken nicht vor Mord und Totschlag zurück, um die geziemende Rangordnung wiederherzustellen.

Die wunderlich wunderbare Symbiose zwischen Mensch und Tier manifestiert sich am deutlichsten, wenn beide zusammenleben. Lear macht Tiere – vor allem Vögel – häufig zu Mit-Bewohnern. Mal nisten acht Vögel im riesigen Bart eines Mannes (1), mal sitzen gleich dreizehn auf der ungeheuer langen Nase eines anderen (111), mal sucht der Mensch Unterkunft bei Tieren. In Limerick Nr. 185 hält sich der Mensch nicht nur im Nest der Eulen auf – er ist einer der Ihren:

Dies ist gar nicht mehr lustig. Der einsame Mensch sucht und findet Zuflucht in einer Vogelfamilie – fern allen menschlichen Kontakten und Bindungen.

Solch düstere Züge finden sich häufig in Lears Limericks, doch nicht immer: Überall nach Abgründigem zu gründeln, wäre albern. In manchen Limericks ist nichts Hintergründiges enthalten: Dort spielt Lear mit der Sprache, dort lässt er seiner Fantasie die Zügel schießen. Bei seinem Spiel hält Lear sich nicht an Regeln – er ist ein Spielverderber.

*Theo Stemmler*

# Inhalt